JOSHUA SLOCUM

The *Spray* in Sydney Harbor, 1897.

JOSHUA SLOCUM

WALTER TELLER

 RUTGERS UNIVERSITY PRESS
New Brunswick   New Jersey

Joshua Slocum is an extensively revised and augmented edition of *The Search for Captain Slocum*.

This is a world in which each of us, knowing his limitations, knowing the evils of superficiality and the terrors of fatigue, will have to cling to what is close to him, to what he knows, to what he can do, to his friends and his tradition and his love, lest he be dissolved in a universal confusion and know nothing and love nothing.

J. Robert Oppenheimer
Prospects in the Arts and Sciences

Books by Walter Teller

The Farm Primer
Roots in the Earth (with P. Alston Waring)
An Island Summer
The Search for Captain Slocum: A Biography
The Voyages of Joshua Slocum
Five Sea Captains
Area Code 215: A Private Line in Bucks County
Cape Cod and the Offshore Islands

Contents

Illustrations

Frontispiece   The *Spray* in Sydney Harbor, 1897

Group I   The Early Voyages

Group II   Documentary

Preface

During the fifteen years that have passed since the first edition of this book was published, Joshua Slocum's name has become more widely known. Further documents pertaining to him have turned up, and more persons with firsthand knowledge of him have come forward. Clearly, the book was ripe for revision. When I began revising, however, I saw that merely fitting in the new matter, and making corrections in the old, would not be enough. Though Slocum's life history remained essentially the same, my many years of living with the material had brought a change in perspective. I found it necessary to reexamine everything I had said earlier, and finally to rewrite the book entirely. Some heretofore unpublished illustrations have been added.

W.T.
Chilmark, Massachusetts
April 1971

From the Preface to the First Edition

The search for Captain Slocum began with a chance reading of his book, *Sailing Alone Around the World,* and a chance discovery that people who knew him were still alive. For Joshua Slocum had disappeared at sea some forty years before; boat, logs, letters, papers, all going down with him.

Living on the edge of the twentieth century, Slocum saw his beloved tall-masted sailing ships driven from the seas by the coming of steam. The world, as he knew it, was changing. But he, personally, would not convert to steam. He shook his fist at progress, defied it, and in the end won a sort of victory.

Fifty-one years old, brown-bearded and bald-headed, Joshua Slocum sailed around the world in a boat he built himself out of a derelict hulk. He sailed without power, radio, money, advertising sponsor, or life insurance; and he went entirely alone. He was the first man known to history to do so.

Slocum pitted himself, his will and skill, against the universe in the time-honored manner of all assailers. He had the strength to live in accordance with his own beliefs, even when they ran counter to prevailing thought. These are qualities that make a man worth searching for.

Beyond all this, he wrote a book which is among the finest ever written by a man who did not set out to be a writer. *Sailing Alone Around the World* has universal appeal. More than fifty years after publication it is still in print in this country and in England. It has been translated into Polish, German, French, Dutch, Swedish, and Italian.

Though Joshua Slocum was that rarest of sea-birds, an articulate Yankee sailor, there was much that he did not, could not, tell. "The voyage . . . ," he wrote, "was the natural outcome not only of my love of adventure, but of my lifelong experience." What was the lifelong experience? What were the forces that shaped him? What made him able to do what he did? How did doing it affect him? I decided to go looking for what clues might be left.

Searching, I visited the house and farm which had been Slocum's one and only home on land. I spoke with his widow, then in her ninetieth year. She said, "I called him Josh, sometimes Joshua, or Captain, if I thought he needed the honor." She added that Slocum spoke his mind freely and that "it did not hurt his feelings to let you know what he was thinking." I held the hand that had held his.

I saw a photograph of him. It was taken on the Massachusetts coast, six years before the end. Slocum is sitting on a homemade bench on his boat, his black felt hat just clearing the boom. He looks spare, flinty, fearless, and yet somehow afraid. I noticed his two shoes were not laced the same way. That was funny. Who would lace one shoe one way, and one the other?

Slocum was a man so tied to a time, and that time so gone, we can surely say he will never live again. With the lapse of a few more years, the testimony of those who knew him will also be lost. One seeks him now in the drifting memories of old men and women, and in such scattered and fragmentary records as survive. Perhaps the search will, after all, throw some light on a man determined to be his own man and, whatever the cost, to live the life he believed in.

Chronological Table

1844	(20 February)	Joshua Slocum born, Nova Scotia.
1852		Family moves to Westport, Brier Island, N.S.
1860		Mother dies. Leaves home and goes to sea.
1862		Promoted to mate on merchant ship.
c. 1865		Becomes a United States citizen.
1869		Master of coasting schooner.
1870	(December)	Captain of bark *Washington* carrying cargo from San Francisco to Sydney, Australia.
1871	(31 January)	Marries Virginia Albertina Walker in Sydney. Bark *Washington* is lost. A new command, the barkentine *Constitution*.
1872	(January)	First child, Victor, born.
1873		Commands the *B. Aymar*.
	(December)	Second son born and named for the ship.
1875	(June)	Daughter, Jessie, born.
c. 1876		Shipbuilding in the Philippines.
c. 1877		Becomes owner of schooner *Pato*. Fishes for cod in North Pacific. Virginia gives birth to twins who die.
c. 1878		Sells *Pato* in Honolulu. Buys *Amethyst*, an older ship but his largest to date.
1879	(June?)	Birth of a daughter who lives a few weeks.
1881	(4 March)	Son, James A. Garfield Slocum, born.
	(23 June)	Becomes master and part-owner of *Northern Light*, after selling *Amethyst*.
1882		Arrives in New York; visited by father and relatives.
	(26 June)	Interviewed by *New York Tribune*.
	(August)	Sails from New York for Yokohama; continues around the world.
1884	(24 January)	Slocum no longer an owner or master of *Northern Light*.
	(4 March)	Buys bark *Aquidneck*. Sails from Baltimore with freight for South America.
	(25 July)	Virginia dies on board *Aquidneck*. Buried in English Cemetery, Buenos Aires.
1886	(22 February)	Slocum marries Henrietta (Hettie) Elliott.
	(28 February)	Slocum, Hettie, Victor, Garfield, leave New York on *Aquidneck* bound for South America.

	(5 May)	Arrives in Montevideo.
1887		Freights in *Aquidneck* along east coast of South America.
	(23 July)	Attacked on board *Aquidneck* in harbor at Antonina, Brazil. Shoots two of his assailants, killing one of them.
	(23 August)	Tried in Brazilian court and acquitted.
	(December)	*Aquidneck* wrecked at Paranagua Bay, Brazil.
1888		Builds 35-foot canoe *Liberdade*.
	(24 June)	Slocum, Hettie, Victor, Garfield, set sail in *Liberdade* from Paranagua Bay, bound for United States.
	(27 December)	Arrives at Washington, D.C.
1889		Writes *Voyage of the Liberdade*.
1890		Publishes at own expense *Voyage of the Liberdade*, Press of Robinson & Stephenson, Boston.
1892		Derelict oyster sloop *Spray* given Slocum by Captain Eben Pierce of Fairhaven, Massachusetts.
	(March)	Begins rebuilding *Spray*.
1893	(April?)	*Spray* launched.
	(7 December)	Leaves New York as "navigator in command" of warship *Destroyer* bound for Brazil.
1894	(13 February)	Reaches Bahia and hands over *Destroyer* to Brazilians.
	(March)	Returns by steamer to Fairhaven.
		Writes *Voyage of the Destroyer from New York to Brazil;* publishes at own expense.
	(September)	One thousand copies of *Voyage of the Liberdade* published by Roberts Brothers, Boston.
1895	(24 April)	Slocum sails from Boston in *Spray*.
	(7 May)	Sails from Gloucester.
	(13 May)	Arrives Nova Scotia.
	(20 July)	Arrives Fayal, Azores.
	(4 August)	Arrives Gibraltar.
	(5 October)	Arrives Pernambuco, Brazil.
	(5 November)	Arrives Rio de Janeiro.
	(December)	Goes aground on coast of Uruguay.
1896	(January)	Sails up Plata River to Buenos Aires.
	(February)	Enters eastern entrance Strait of Magellan.
	(26 April)	Arrives Juan Fernandez.
	(16 July)	Arrives Samoa.
	(9 October)	Arrives Sydney.
	(December)	At Melbourne.
1897		Visits Tasmania. Gives first travel lecture.
	(August)	Arrives at Keeling Cocos Islands. On way home.

	(17 November)	At Port Natal, South Africa.
1898	(January)	At Capetown.
	(26 March)	Sails from Capetown.
	(11 April)	Arrives St. Helena.
	(22 May)	Arrives Grenada, West Indies.
	(27 June)	Arrives Newport, Rhode Island.
	(3 July)	Ties up at Fairhaven.
1899	(September)	First installment of *Sailing Alone Around the World* published in *Century Illustrated Monthly Magazine.*
1900	(March)	Abridgment of *Voyage of the Destroyer* published by *McClure's* magazine.
	(24 March)	*Sailing Alone Around the World* published in book form by Century Company, New York.
		Sailing Alone Around the World published by Sampson Low, Marston & Co., London.
1901	(May–November)	Slocum and *Spray* at Pan-American Exposition, Buffalo.
		Writes, publishes and sells *Sloop Spray Souvenir.*
1902	(March)	Buys farm at West Tisbury, Massachusetts, on Martha's Vineyard.
	(October)	"The Man Who Sailed Alone Around the World in a Thirty-seven-foot Boat" by Clifton Johnson, illustrated, appears in *Outing* magazine.
	(November)	First installment of *Voyage of the Liberdade,* abridged, appears in *Outing* magazine under the title of "Voyage of the Aquidneck and Its Varied Adventures in South American Waters."
1903	(February)	"The Cook Who Sailed Alone" by Clifton Johnson published in *Good Housekeeping* magazine.
		Around the World in the Sloop Spray, A Geographical Reader . . . published by Charles Scribner's Sons, New York, for school use.
1905	(November)	Sails alone in *Spray* from Martha's Vineyard bound for West Indies.
1906	(March)	"Bully Hayes, the Last Buccaneer, Written from Data Supplied by Captain Joshua Slocum" published by *Outing* magazine.
	(April)	Sails from West Indies, bound north.
	(May)	Arrested in Riverton, New Jersey.
	(August)	Entertained at Sagamore Hill by President Theodore Roosevelt.
	(November)	Sails from Martha's Vineyard for West Indies.

1907   (May)   Calls on Roosevelt at White House.
        (November?)   Sets out on third voyage alone in *Spray* for West
                              Indies.
1908   (June)   Delivers two-ton coral tree found in Bahamas to
                              American Museum of Natural History, New
                              York.
1909   (14 November)   Sets sail from Tisbury (Vineyard Haven), Mas-
                              sachusetts, bound for South America.
1924   (15 January)   Joshua Slocum declared legally dead as of 14
                              November 1909.

Part I

1

*the wonderful sea
charmed me from the first*

"I was born in a cold spot, on coldest North Mountain, on a cold February 20th," Joshua Slocum wrote. Chilling was the scene, and sea-haunted. It overlooked the worn coast and tremendous tides of the Bay of Fundy. Fogs rolled in from the ocean ceaselessly. The year was 1844.

In those days, the Canadian maritime province of Nova Scotia was one of the shipbuilding centers of the world, a place dedicated to the sea, and to the modes of life peculiar to sea-faring men. ". . . it is nothing against the master mariner if the birth-place mentioned on his certificate be Nova Scotia," was how Slocum put it. Although, as he said, his people "on both sides . . . were sailors," actually his father was a farmer, and it was on a farm that he spent his early years—though within sight and sound of the Bay.

History had put him in this spot. An early John Slocombe * of Massachusetts had been a Quaker, opposed to war. After the War of Independence, he was exiled, along with thousands of others

* "Slocomb, or Slocum. The name, like so many English surnames, is of local origin, and due to the abundant growth of the sloe tree, or wild plum, in some *valley* or *depression among the hills,* called in Old English a *combe.* A person, say, Richard, living in such a spot would become known among outsiders as 'Richard of the *sloe combe,*' and when the use of surnames became general, his posterity would inherit the name crystallized into its modern form. Our Slocombs derive from SIMON, who married at Wrentham, Mass., in 1719. (He no doubt was a lineal descendant from Anthony Slocum, one of the first purchasers of Taunton, Mass., in 1637.)" Calnek, W. A., edited by Savary, A. W., *History of the County of Annapolis,* Toronto, 1897, p. 601.

who had sided with England or had remained neutral. But because his father and uncle had captained transports from Boston to Quebec for the Loyalists, John Slocombe's exile was softened by a grant of land from the king: 500 acres on a trap ridge in Wilmot Township, Annapolis County, Nova Scotia. There John's progeny lived and there Joshua was born.

As a small boy working on "the old clay farm which some calamity" had made his father's, Joshua heard the roaring of the forty-foot Fundy tides, the highest in the world. He heard the deep summons of the sea. On clear days he saw the New Brunswick shore across the Bay. From the ridge, he looked down and saw tall spruce trees good for building ships. A mile or so down the slope stood a grist mill and mill pond. Joshua built a raft of spruce fence rails with boards nailed across. Rigging up a mast and sail, he cruised over the pond before the breeze. He had to pole his way back. Whenever he could, he joined in with neighbors fishing for cod and mackerel.

Though the view from the farm was superb, the soil was poor. Joshua's father seems to have inherited the unproductive part of the grant. The rich valley lands had gone to others. It was a hard life but it had flavor; and if the two-story shingled farmhouse, still standing, was plain indeed, its hearth and hearth-fire were to be remembered. "What good things came from those old fire-places —oh! those barley cakes, and those buckwheat flapjacks—oh!" Joshua Slocum recalled many years later.

But the means of even this simple subsistence was not easy to come by. The family was large. "Poor father!" Joshua wrote long afterwards, "what a load he carried and how he grubbed a living, for us all, out of the old clay farm. And how I've seen him break down when he came back to the 'Family Alter' . . . and cry Father, Father. . . ."

John Slocombe was a big man, six feet tall, two hundred pounds, and muscular. "He was not afraid of a capful of wind, and he never took a back seat at a camp meeting, or a good, old-fashioned revival," his son recalled. An old-style Methodist deacon of his church, and much concerned with the devil, he preached a religion as bleak as the surrounding fog-banks. "I never cared much for the devil after I grew up and got away to sea . . . I myself, do not care much for your long-faced tyrannical Christian," Joshua wrote long after.

When Joshua was eight, the family left the homestead and the field where several generations of Slocombes lay buried and moved down country to the village of Westport on Brier Island. Brier Island, off the northwest corner of Digby Neck, is tiny, only four miles long. On the north and west it is bounded by the Bay of Fundy. Its south shore is washed by St. Mary's Bay. It was a place apart when the Slocombes went there, and even now the small raft-like ferries make only two trips a day to the mainland. The Slocombes went because they were in trouble. Sarah, the mother, was ailing. John, the father, having failed at farming, hoped to make a living in the village.

Sarah Jane Sothern, Joshua's mother, was the daughter of the keeper of the Southwest Point Light at Westport, which faced the Atlantic and guarded the entrance to the Bay of Fundy. Westport tradition says that the Sotherns, retired naval people, were a shade more polished than the up-country Slocombes, and that Sarah was more cultivated than her husband. Seriously ill, Sarah wanted to return to the village where she had been born and where she could be near her kin. She was tired, "too many children coming too closely," a relative wrote, "dear Sarah, so frail, and the babies demanding so much care . . . a lovely, gentle soul." Very little is known about Sarah Jane. She was eighteen when she married John, Joshua's father; he was twenty-one. There are no details of her life after that except for the list, the familiar list, in front of the family Bible:

> Sarah Jane, born 18 November, 1834; died 5 Sept., 1853.
> Elizabeth, born 7 July, 1837.
> John Ingraham, born 28 July 1839; died 10 Oct., 1844.
> Georgiana, born 5 September, 1841.
> Joshua, b. 20 Feb., 1844.
> Margaret, born 11 August, 1846.
> Ornan, b. 10 June, 1849.
> Alice, born 26 May, 1851.
> Henrietta, born 26 April, 1854.
> Ingram Bill, born 6 November, 1856.
> Ella, born 5 February, 1860.

A few days after Ella, the eleventh child, was born, Sarah Jane died. The tombstone, so often the only record of a woman of her time and station having existed at all, read, "To the memory of

Sarah Jane, wife of John Slocombe, died Feb. 16, 1860, being 46 years old."

Joshua was the fifth child and could not have had much mothering. From the beginning he was a competitor in the struggle for survival. A brother died the year he was born, a sister arrived two years later. Three more years, and another baby arrived. And after that, another, another, another, and still another.

"As for myself, the wonderful sea charmed me from the first," Joshua Slocum wrote long after. "At the age of eight I had already been afloat with other boys on the bay, with chances greatly in favor of being drowned." This was hardly an overstatement. The Bay of Fundy is rightly dreaded by men in small boats. Its tide goes out suddenly, silently, leaving the ocean floor naked, only to come raging back, full of fury and menace. Joshua, like most boys and sailors of his time, could not swim. But even today not many who grow up in Westport know how; the water is too cold to learn to swim. Though Joshua did not swim, he had no fear of the water. He did not tangle with it but respected and understood it in a way that the swimmer, who fights against it, does not. He was fatalistic about it. He knew that the sea would claim him if it meant to, and in a sense, he was willing to accept death in it.

After giving up on the farm and moving to Westport on Brier Island, John Slocombe opened a harborside shop where he made fishermen's cowhide boots. He knew the trade; he had made boots and shoes as a sideline while farming. There were vats of soaking high-smelling leather to tend as well as the cutting, sewing, and pegging of bootsoles with hand-whittled pegs. He needed help. So Joshua, ten years old, was taken from school. By this time Joshua had had at most three years of one-room schooling. It is not surprising the future circumnavigator and writer never learned to spell or punctuate.

From the boot shop Joshua looked out on the harbor where fishing and trading boats came and went, and beyond to the Bay where the larger sailing ships passed. The work within he disliked intensely. Father and son did not get along.

The break between them came over a trivial matter, as it usually does in such cases; but it was symbolic and never forgotten. Joshua, now twelve, had been caught in the cellar, "putting the finishing touches on a ship model which had taken him many furtive moments to make. His father burst in upon him in a fury, seized the precious work of art (and hope) and dashed it to the ground, smashing yards and masts and utterly destroying the whole thing . . . The strange part of all this cruelty on the part of the elder Slocombe was that it was never greatly resented by his son Josh who rather regarded it as a just exercise of parental authority. However, he regretted the smashing of the ship model more than he did the castigation." In after years, he used to "tell his mates about it at the cabin table. They thought it was pretty rough," Joshua's oldest son wrote in a biography of his father.

When he was fourteen, Joshua ran away, and for a short time was cook on a fishing schooner, "but I was not long in the galley," he wrote, "for the crew mutinied at the appearance of my first duff, and 'chucked me out' before I had a chance to shine as a culinary artist." When he returned, the escapade cost him a thrashing.

But like many men, once he got away, Joshua was proud of his father, and of the tyranny he had endured. In his book he wrote, "My father was the sort of man who, if wrecked on a desert island, could find his way home if he had a jack knife and could find a tree." But whatever Joshua had inherited from his father, he did not look like him. Rather, he had the "finely cut features and unusual eyes" of his mother, to whom he never referred. On the basis of the meager facts one can only speculate as to why he found it so difficult to mention his mother, or later, his wife. Was it because he depended so much on the women he loved that when they died, part of him died with them? If his mother gave him encouragement against the hardships of his childhood, and in his troubles with his father, the irreparable loss of the supportiveness he required—the death and separation which afterwards would be repeated with his wife—such things could have made him virtually unable to speak of the women important to him. While his mother lived, he made only one attempt to escape. When she died, Joshua left Westport and Brier Island for good.

A hundred and one years later, in 1961, the Government of Nova Scotia, and the Joshua Slocum Society of the United States, unveiled a cairn at Westport. Mounted on the cairn was a bronze plaque inscribed with these words: "In Honor of Captain Joshua Slocum / The First Man to Sail Around the World Alone . . . /

He was Born on North Mountain . . . / Lived at Westport Until
He Went to Sea in 1860 . . ."

Joshua was 16 when he and a friend named Cheny shipped
from St. John as foremast hands on a deal drogher, a slow, clumsy
lumber-carrying sailing vessel, bound for Dublin. Was this the
moment when he changed the spelling of his surname from
Slocombe to Slocum? Or did the change come later when he became an American citizen? Victor Slocum (Joshua's oldest son)
wrote that on sailing day Joshua and Cheny were the only sober
hands on board. They were earnest young men who saved their
money. In due course both became masters. Joshua, according to
his son, neither drank nor smoked. Furthermore, he studied whenever he could. Practicing taking sights with the sextant, and teach-
ing himself navigation from a copy of J. W. Norie's *Epitome of
Navigation,* Joshua was a natural student. And he had a kind of
genius too. His interest ran narrow and deep.

From Dublin, Joshua sailed to Liverpool; and from Liverpool to
China, via the Cape of Good Hope. He made the latter passage on
a British ship, the *Tanjore,* and remembered it, later, without love.
"I may have been a little severe on Captain M of the old 'Tanjore'
but it is my only revenge for years of broken health brought on
by the Captain 'who talked through his nose' having us, his sailors,
working the ice cargo in the cool of the mornings and evenings
and then aloft or, worse still, over the ship's side in the heat of
the days, which in Hong Kong in the summer, as it was, was
intensely hot several of the crew died. I could not stand it, but
when I left the ship I sued—and recovered three months extra
wages. The crime for which the crew was so inhumanly worked,
was that each had the high wages of our home port—$50 per
month."

In *Sailing Alone,* he remembered Captain Martin as a first-rate
navigator, but an officer so imperious and brass-bound that he
could not hand ordinary seaman Slocum a letter but "gave it to the
first mate; the first mate gave it to the second mate, and he laid
it, michingly, on the capstan head, where I could get it!"

From Hong Kong, the *Tanjore* sailed to Batavia, present-day
Jakarta, Indonesia, where young Joshua was left in a hospital
ashore, down with fever. Trials and hard treatment, however, did
not change his mind as to how he intended to spend his life.

2

toward the goal
of happiness

A sharp distinction existed on British ships of those days between
foremast hands like Joshua Slocum and young men who signed on
as apprentices. Apprentices got to be officers by paying a premium
and then serving a prescribed time. Foremast hands, by contrast,
had no way to promotion except ability. The class distinction
extended to sleeping and eating quarters. Apprentices berthed
in the cabin aft. Foremast hands bunked in the forecastle forward of the mast and near the bow of the vessel. Joshua Slocum
was always proud of having come up the hard way; " 'over the
bows,' and not in through the cabin windows," was how he
phrased it.

He was 18 and on a voyage from Liverpool to the Dutch East
Indies when he won promotion to mate, a key step upward. He
became first mate not long after. In his new capacity he twice
sailed around Cape Horn in British ships, trading coal out and
grain home—between Liverpool, Cardiff, and San Francisco.
Joshua was a "husky youth"—weighed 180 pounds—wrote his
oldest son, Victor.

In 1864, when in the middle of the Atlantic, on the bark *Agra*,
Joshua had a very close call. He was on the upper topsail
yard, gathering in sail, when a gust struck and pitched him
off. "His fall was broken and his life saved by collision with the
main yard, which he struck on his head, cutting a gash over his
left eye," reads an old newspaper account. The scar remained.

When Joshua Slocum made San Francisco again he decided to
call it his hailing port and to become a citizen of the United

States, "a naturalized Yankee," as he said. In those years, the
1860s, when the transcontinental railroad was being completed,
San Francisco was expanding into a famous city as well as chief
seaport of the West Coast, open to every kind of excitement and
enterprise. Fortunes were being made; Joshua decided to try for
his in the salmon fishery. He headed north and with a partner
built a boat on the Columbia River. Boatbuilding as well as seafaring fascinated him. "Next in attractiveness, after seafaring, came
ship-building. I longed to be master in both professions . . . ," he
wrote. Though from time to time Slocum would turn to fishing,
catching fish was not his goal. Salmon fishing did not last long.
His next enterprise was hunting sea otters near Vancouver Island
off British Columbia.

Victor Slocum wrote, "My father kept a journal covering this
period spent on the Columbia River, Gray's Harbor, Puget Sound,
and British Columbia, but I remember only parts of it . . . his
own camp life . . . references to the sea otter and the smaller
fur-bearing animals . . . humorous allusions . . ." None of this
journal has come to light, but apparently Slocum, despite little
schooling, began writing early in his career.

These inshore adventures did not hold his interest; his real
ambition was command of a ship. In 1869 he achieved it. At age
25 he became captain of a coasting schooner plying between San
Francisco and Seattle. It was a young age at which to become a
master but not unusual in his time and profession. Victor Slocum,
the only one of Joshua's three sons to follow the sea, wrote, "The
recognition of worth on the sea is very sure, no doubt because of
so little competition."

Captain Joshua's next command, the bark *Washington*, 332 tons,
was a further step upward. In December 1870 she sailed from
San Francisco for Sydney, Australia, with a general cargo. From
Sydney, she was to sail to Cook Inlet, Alaska, where Slocum again
was to fish for salmon.

But something of moment happened in Sydney; Slocum got
married. It is typical of him never to have mentioned where or
how he met his wife. Once again, the words are lost; only the facts
remain. They were married.

"I, James Greenwood, being Minister of the Bathurst St. Baptist
Church, Sydney, do hereby Certify, that I have this day, at 56

Upper Fort Street, Sydney, duly celebrated Marriage between Joshua Slocum, Bachelor, Master Mariner of Massachusetts,* United States and Virginia Albertina Walker, Spinster, of 19 Buckingham Street, Strawberry Hill, Sydney, after Declaration duly made as by law required. Dated this 31st day of January, 1871 . . .

"The Consent of Mr. Wm. Henry Walker, 19 Buckingham Street, Strawberry Hill, Sydney, was given to the Marriage of Virginia Albertina Walker with Joshua Slocum, the said Virginia Albertina Walker being under the age of Twenty-one years."

Virginia's father, William Walker, was a Forty-niner who had wandered from New York, to California, to the gold mines of Australia, and had finally gone into business in Sydney. Her sister "became a contralto and sang in opera," and she had a younger brother named George.

As so often happened in the romances of sea captains of that day, the young lady, who generally knew her husband perhaps one, two, or three weeks, picked herself up, packed her belongings, kissed mother and father good-bye, stepped aboard her new husband's ship, and sailed away forever. That is what Virginia did. She was, however, spectacularly well-suited to the strenuous life she had chosen.

She was born on Staten Island, New York. On her mother's side she descended from the Leni-Lenape of that region. Her second son, B. Aymar Slocum, wrote me she was proud of her Indian blood. She loved the outdoors; as a girl in Australia she "was trained to ride horses and on weekends, she rode with associates into the Blue Mountains, exploring and sleeping on the ground much as the natives did. She told of cooking eggs in a piece of cloth and held in a boiling hot spring. I remember seeing her riding equipment which she always had with her aboard ship, also the whip."

If the bark *Washington* resembled other ships of its class and date, the quarters Virginia now moved into were constraining, to put it mildly. The living accommodations for the captain generally consisted of a damp and airless cabin which contained a large

---

* Though sailing out of San Francisco, Slocum was, by ancestry and affinity, a Massachusetts man. He had no home. His mailing address was with one or another of his sisters.

desk, barometer, chronometers, a sofa, and, in the case of Slocum, probably many books. The only light came from a transom through which Virginia might have an excellent view of the legs of the man at the wheel, and perhaps a little sky beyond, criss-crossed by the ship's rigging. In spite of tight quarters a piano was sometimes squeezed in. How important it must have been to hear music on the long voyages.

The sleeping quarters were a stateroom aft, largely taken up by a bed so swung as to counteract the rocking of the vessel. There was room for a trunk and washstand and a wife, if she chose to accompany her husband, but most masters sailed alone. This cabin and stateroom was partitioned off from the saloon, amidships, which opened onto the cubby-holes occupied by the mates, and the galley. Into this tiny space would crowd the captain, the exceptional wife, and the mates, for meal after meal, day after day, month after month, on the long voyages. In general, ships of this sort were no place for women, and crews resented the presence of the captain's wife aboard, even though in some cases, by their good sportsmanship and usefulness—(some mended and cared for the sick, and sometimes, like Virginia, became very adequate navigators)—they won the respect of the men. It was a rarely courageous wife who accompanied her husband on more than one voyage. But Virginia, for the rest of her life, sailed wherever Joshua went. It was also a rarely demanding sea captain who expected his wife to share the hardships and dangers of his profession, and who in his daily life required her by his side.

The honeymoon trip across the vast Pacific, from Sydney in the southwest to Cook Inlet, Alaska, in the northeast, in search of salmon, might have been enough to dissuade a less hardy girl. As Slocum's oldest son later put it, "The fishing was carried out successfully except for the loss of the vessel." It was only four years since Russia had sold Alaska to the United States and the waters were not well known to American masters. The charts were still very sketchy. The *Washington* dragged her anchors in a gale and was stranded on the shoals, some 200 miles from Kodiak. This caused "an awkward problem" in the transportation of the salmon. A boat larger than the ship's dories was needed.

Thereupon, the captain and his three mates fell to and built a 35-foot whaleboat, but just as it was finished, a revenue cutter appeared. Virginia was taken aboard and on to Kodiak and thus spared the open-boat voyage across the icy waters.

Slocum, however, stayed by his doomed vessel while the catch was prepared for shipping. He then used the whaleboat to transport the fish to a couple of sealers with empty holds. The sealers took the salmon to San Francisco, while the captain, his wife, and crew, got passage home on a Russian bark.

The owners of the *Washington,* though they had lost their ship, were apparently satisfied with the master. They gave him another command, the barkentine *Constitution,* a small packet running between San Francisco and Honolulu. This must have been considered ideal by Captain Slocum's young wife. Honolulu, at that time, was a rendezvous for all ships wandering the Pacific, the maritime equivalent of the general store and post-office. It was a social oasis for the painfully isolated and usually very lonely captains' wives. Here one could bring out of the damp trunk the good Sunday dress, press out its two-month or six-month-old wrinkles, and stroll about the streets, or drink tea with friends on the lawn of the hotel. Here a lady could shop for dress goods, discuss patterns, and enjoy that rarest of luxuries—female companionship.

3

*sailed as freighter
and trader*

Virginia gave birth to her first child on board the *Constitution* lying at anchor in San Francisco harbor in 1872. It was a year, almost to the day, since she had married. The baby was a boy, and the proud young parents called him Victor.

The following year, Slocum was put in command of the *B. Aymar*, a full rigged, single topsail, East Indies trader, sailing from Sydney to Amoy. The ship was named after the commercial house that owned her, Ben Aymar & Co. A second son, born on board, at the end of that year, was named after the ship, and like the ship, known as B. Aymar. A third child, Jessie, named for Virginia's sister back home in Australia, was also born on board in June 1875 while the ship lay in Philippine waters. Soon thereafter, the *B. Aymar* was sold in Manila.

In Manila, Slocum took time out to ply his second trade, that of shipbuilder. He met a British marine architect, Edward Jackson, and contracted to build a steamship hull for him. For this purpose, Slocum set up a primitive boatyard at Olongapo, a jungle village at the head of Subic Bay, sixty miles from Manila. The site had advantages. There was plentiful and excellent timber on the nearby mountainside, and there was a natural launching beach. But there were some disadvantages, too: the heavy damp air of a monsoon tropical climate, the reptile-infested beach, poisonous plants, and unfriendly local contractors who resented the successful foreign bidder.

Slocum, who always kept his family with him, had a nipa-thatched house built for his wife and children. The sills were seven feet off the ground, high enough for safety and health, and to provide accommodations for chickens and pigs below. Even so, "centipedes and scorpions had a habit of crawling into our clothes and getting into our shoes . . . it was routine to shake and search everything while dressing . . . ," Victor recalled. Virginia's early camping experiences stood by her now as she made the best of jungle life for herself and her three young children.

The Slocums lived at Olongapo a year. Shipbuilding is slow work. Trees had to be felled and hewn into square logs with axes. Water buffalo then dragged them down to the shore to be ripped into scantling and plank by Tagalog sawyers with hand saws. But in spite of difficulties, which included plots to attack the family and wreck the ship, the 80-ton hull was built, launched, and towed to Manila, to be fitted to the engine. As part of his payment, Slocum was given the *Pato,* designed and built by the same Mr. Jackson and lying nearby in the Pasig River. In one of his earliest extant letters (3 May 1890) Slocum described the *Pato* as "a schooner 45 tons regest." He also pointed out that "Pato is Spanish for duck."

At first, Slocum had no plans for the schooner, but his family (Victor wrote) "agreed that it was better to live afloat in however small a craft," than on the beach at Olongapo. So they picked up some inter-island trips, and then a charter to salvage the cargo of a British bark which was hanging on a reef in the China Sea. After that he decided to try fishing again.

Slocum now made a voyage, as he wrote in the same letter, "from Manilla to Honolulu Via, Hong Kong, Yookohoma, Kamchtacka and the Okotsk Sea, where we filled up with codfish having for outfits in the beginning one splitting knife, the rest we gathered togather as we voyaged along from port to port finally meeting with the Constitution—laden with salt—from which I procured the salt necessary for the cureing of the fish that we set about catching now and which we carried into Oregon, it being the first cargo that ever entered the State. The Constitution . . . on which Victor first saw the light . . . ."

"The whole voyage would be quite a story

"Two of my children were borne on this voyage while at Petropolanska; they were two months old when we arrived at Oregon—4 days old when we began to take in fish

"The whole voyage was a great success . . . .

"Yes Sir we had a stirring voyage and altogether a delightful time on the fishing grounds for every codfish that came in over the rail was a quarter of a dollar—clear— . . . ."

Slocum's letter needs filling in. With the *Pato,* he became a shipowner as well as shipmaster. In his new command, a vessel halfway in size between the *Pir.a* and the *Nina,* with Virginia and their three children, ages about five, four and two, and a crew of sea hunters, he left Manila, crossed the South China Sea, sailed thence to Yokohama, and to the peninsula of Kamchatka and Petropovlovsk-Kamchatski. There, thousands of ocean miles away from all she had known, Virginia gave birth to twins. Four days later, Slocum and his family were on the Okhotsk Grounds, so-called, fishing for cod.

The newly discovered North Pacific cod banks were teeming with fish. Slocum had not brought salt enough to cure a bonanza catch, but he was in luck anyway. In that far-off corner of the world, sailor-like he met an old friend, the *Constitution,* the San Francisco-to-Honolulu packet he formerly commanded and the vessel on which Victor had been born. The *Constitution,* filled with fish, was about to jettison her unused salt. Instead, it was shoveled into the *Pato's* hold. Victor wrote that two weeks saw the *Pato* loaded with 25,000 cod salted down. She then headed for the West Coast.

The twins were two months old when Slocum made Portland and sold his cargo. From Portland he sailed to Honolulu where he and his family ended their 8,000-mile cruise. The above is the only letter I know in which Slocum mentions the *Pato,* and the two children born on that voyage. He does not say they were twins, but his son, B. Aymar, in a letter wrote me they were and that they died in infancy. "The ocean is no place to raise a family," was his quiet comment. Why did Slocum, unlike other sea captains, attempt it? He said of the voyage of the *Pato,* "quite a story"; did he think of writing it? Though his family lost out, the trip paid off. Slocum called it "a great success."

An unscheduled race in Honolulu harbor gave Slocum his chance to sell the *Pato.* One day, according to Victor, the *Pato* was casting off her lines when a sack of mail was rushed down to the wharf. The fast mail schooner had already left. Slocum offered to solve the problem. "Heave aboard here, and I'll take it out to her," he ordered. The mail was handed over and Slocum sailed off in pursuit. Driving the *Pato* at top speed, he overtook the mail ship, blanketed her, and tossed her the sack.

"The race at Honolulu in which the Pato won was very exciting," he wrote in the letter quoted above. "The whole town turning out to see it—

"I sold the Pato soon after for $5000. all in twenty dollar gold pieces, ugh! if I had them now."

Slocum never mentions what family life on board was like, the hardships endured, or the price paid in personal living. Several things, perhaps, account for this; Victorian reticence, the traditional apartness of the sea captain's life, and painful memories. Virtually all that is known of Virginia and her life on board ship comes from letters her children wrote me.

Virginia sewed, played the piano, and reared her children. She also displayed some unusual, and curiously fortunate, abilities: "To spend a few hours with sharks, in mid ocean, when they were present, Mother and I teamed up," B. Aymar recollected. "It was my job to get the shark interested in coming close up. I used a new tin can with a string on it to attract the shark close under the stern where Mother dispatched it with her .32 cal. revolver with which she never needed but one shot. How I loved to see her do it—and without any signs on her part of showing superior skill." Rather unusual memories for a boy to have of his mother, and unusual even for captains' wives. Virginia and her son, B. Aymar, were the only members of the family who could swim. B. Aymar adds that "she was an excellent cook of the rough and ready sort."

It is hard to imagine a more perfect wife for Joshua Slocum. Many years later, after she had died, B. Aymar remembered his father looking at a photograph. "Tears streamed over his face. Finally he said, 'Your mother had the eyes of an eagle and she even saw things I could never see.' Mother's eyes were a brilliant golden color—I have seen such eyes on our Golden Eagles—she knew how to use them, too, but very calmly."

The *Pato* sold, Slocum and his family returned to San Francisco by steamer. In San Francisco, Slocum bought the packet *Amethyst,* a full-rigged vessel of 350 tons register. This was not considered a small ship, and she was Slocum's largest to date. Built in

Massachusetts by the renowned shipbuilder Thatcher Magoun, and launched in 1822, she was one of the oldest American ships afloat.* The captain fitted her out for the Philippines-to-China timber trade.

On the first voyage with the *Amethyst*, Slocum carried cargo and passengers to Manila. In addition to his family, he took along his brother Ingram, as cook, and his sister Ella, to help his wife. It was proving a very strenuous life for Virginia. "I believe that she had a weak heart," B. Aymar wrote. "She often fainted when trouble disturbed her."

In July, Slocum made arrangements for carrying timber from the hardwood forests in the Province of Tayabas, in lower Luzon. B. Aymar recollected that while the *Amethyst* rode at anchor in Tayabas Bay, two natives paddled out with eggs, jungle fowl, fruit, and a boa constrictor, with its tail tied to an outrigger. The captain wanted to take the lot. He was assured that the snake, tied by his dangerous end, was safe. But Virginia was not convinced, and she got Joshua to give up the notion of buying the specimen. "Anything to make a dollar, danger or no," wrote B. Aymar. "Father was a trader in any line."

For several years the *Amethyst* carried all manner of freight, timber from the hardwood forests of the Philippines, coal from Nagasaki to Vladivostok and Shanghai, natural ice from Hakodate to Hong Kong, gunpowder from Shanghai to Tainan. Somewhere in all this voyaging and sometime in 1879, Virginia gave birth to another daughter, but the infant died soon after. Virginia wrote her mother in Australia about it—the only letter from her hand that I know of.

Laguemanac. Philippine Islands
July 17/1879

Dearest Mother & all

You must excuse for writing you so short a letter. I have been verey sick ever since the 15 of last month I feel a little better now it is such a strange sicken(?). I have not been able to eat anything till lately. Dear Josh has got me every thing he can think of my hand shakes so

---

* In Chinese waters, the *Amethyst* was known as "Old 1822" because of the Roman numerals rather than her name on her burgee. In her, according to the *New York Daily Tribune*, 26 June 1882, p. 8, "Captain Slocum feared he would end his seafaring career in a typhoon in the China sea . . . ."

now I can hardley write. Dear Mother my Dear little baby died the other day & I expect that is partley the cause. every time her teeth would start to come she would cry all night if I would cut them through the gum would grow togather again. the night she died she had one convulsion after another I gave her a hot bath and some medecine & was quite quiet infact I thought she was going to come around when she gave a quiet sigh and was gone. Dear Josh embalmed her in brandy for we would not leave her in this horid place she did look so pretty after she died Dearest Mother I canot write any more

/s/   Virginia

On the next page Virginia wrote in the corner, "Victor's letter." The boy had written:

July 17/1879

Dear Granmama

We are going to Japan. I am tired of this place. I hope you are well and Granapapa Aunt Jessie and Uncle George. good bye from Victor

Late in 1880, Slocum sailed into Hong Kong. The harbor was crowded with ships. There were no tugs. In a letter to me, B. Aymar recalled, "Father ordered 'all hands stand by all stations,' including the anchor which the first mate had to attend to.

"Try to picture the *Amethyst* under full sail heading for a narrow passageway between three British warships on the starboard side and a full rigged merchant ship on the port side.

"When these anchored vessels saw the *Amethyst* bearing down on that narrow waterway between them, their crews expected to see a very severe smashup of at least three vessels.

"Father took the wheel—mother stood by him. Her silence gave him confidence. He wished to reach an anchorage in the middle of the entire fleet before him.

"The admiral of one of IIer Majesty's Ships stood at his station looking for a crash of spars and torn sails. Father just cleared the H.M.S. by inches—then skilfully cleared the merchant ship by a few inches—passed on to the vacancy and with 'down helm' swung into the wind, and the 'let go the anchor' order was given. It was then that father remembered his breach of marine etiquette for he did not salute the H.M.S. in passing . . . .

"Father wrote an apology to the admiral whose reply read like this—'Any man who can sail a ship under full sail through a passageway too dangerous to contemplate need not apologize to the entire British Navy. You are hereby invited to join me aboard the H.M.S. (date given) and the lady who stood beside you on that occasion.' Signed by the admiral.

"That may give you a picture of the strength my mother had and of her judgment valued by Father—one peep from her would have changed the whole picture."

As always, Virginia stood by Slocum.

4

the magnificent ship

Virginia gave birth to her last child, a son, 3 March 1881, on board the *Amethyst* in Hong Kong harbor. March 4th was Inauguration Day in America. The parents, far from their native and adopted land, honored the incoming president by naming the baby James A. Garfield Slocum. They called him Garfield. Not many weeks after his birth, Joshua, Virginia and their four children moved into larger quarters.

The move came about this way. An American ship, the *Northern Light,* happened to be in Hong Kong harbor at the same time as the *Amethyst.* The two vessels contrasted strongly. The *Amethyst* was almost sixty years old, the *Northern Light* only eight. The *Northern Light,* built in 1873 in Quincy, Massachusetts, by George Thomas, had three masts, three decks, a round stern, and sported a figurehead. She was 220 feet long, 43 feet wide, 20 feet deep and measured 1,857 tons—five times the size of the *Amethyst.* Then and there Slocum made his big trade. He sold the *Amethyst* and bought shares in the larger ship. On 23 June 1881, at Hong Kong, Joshua Slocum became master of the *Northern Light* (Official No. 18749)—so say the records in the National Archives, Washington, D.C.

"The magnificent ship," and "his best command" is how Slocum described the *Northern Light.* "I had a right to be proud of her," he wrote, "for at that time—in the 1880s—she was the finest American sailing vessel afloat." Slocum, 37 years old, had struggled to the top of the tree.

After taking command in Hong Kong, Slocum sailed to Manila, where he took on a cargo of sugar which he then carried west-

ward, around the Cape of Good Hope, to Liverpool. By the time
he and his family sailed into New York, the *Northern Light's*
home port, it was summer of 1882. He had brought his ship half
way around the world. And a profitable voyage it had been for
master and owners.

Command of the square-rigged *Northern Light* * marked the
high point of Slocum's professional commercial career. All he had
set out to do he had done. He was captain and part-owner of a
tall-masted ship. He was making money in the Pacific trade. He
loved the wife who companioned him on his voyages and bore
his children. Standing now in his prime—dangers and gambles
behind him—Slocum wanted his father to see what he, the son,
had accomplished.

Father and son had not met since the day when young Joshua
had left Nova Scotia. Twenty-two years had passed since then.
Now, like Joseph in Egypt, sending for Jacob, Slocum, in New
York, asked that his aging parent come see his son in his glory.
He sent the old man the money for the trip, for John Slocombe
still was a fiscal failure: The old farmer, remarried and now
retired—he was past seventy—obeyed the summons, and took along
a daughter of his second family. He had never seen his daughter-
in-law, Virginia, nor the four grandchildren.

"Father came down to see me in my fine ship *Northern Light*,"
Joshua wrote years later to a cousin, "but we didn't spend our
time talking about fine large ships, our business was a quarter
of a century back—just—'Joshua' said he 'do you remember the
night in the little boat when we rowed all night on a lee-shore
and the fishing vessels came into port with close reefed sail?'

"Didn't I remember it!"

Quite possibly, father and son never saw each other again.
John Slocombe died 9 September 1887, while the captain was
away on another voyage.

The *Northern Light* lay at pier 23, East River, a short way
above the still uncompleted Brooklyn Bridge. The ship's rig was
so lofty part of it had to be struck to let her pass under the

---

* Slocum's *Northern Light*, which he called "as beautiful as her name,"
should not be confused with an earlier clipper ship, also named *Northern
Light*. The latter, designed by Samuel Pook, was built at South Boston in
1851. By Slocum's time the day of the clipper had gone.

span designed to accommodate steamers. Steam was tightening its grip, and ships like the *Northern Light* were fast becoming outmoded. Those were the final hours when masts and rigging in geometric patterns towered over the city. While Slocum was reaching a personal zenith, the sun was setting on the long age of sail.

A reporter for the *New York Tribune* went aboard. Writing of "An American Home Afloat," he described this "typical American ship, commanded by a typical American sailor who has a typical American wife to accompany him on his long voyages, and to make his cabin as acceptable a home as he could have on shore. No one, to look at the graceful lines of this vessel, her Yankee rigging and sails, her bold cutwater and her noble stern, could mistake her for any other than an American ship. . . . A visit to her deck suggests two sad and striking thoughts, one that American sailing ships are becoming obsolete and the other that so few American sailors can be found. . . . The tautness, trimness, and cleanliness of this vessel, from keelson to truck and from stem to stern, are features not common on merchant ships. The neat canvas cover over the steering-wheel bearing the vessel's name and hailing port, worked with silk, is the handiwork of the captain's wife. Descending to the main cabin, one wonders whether or not he is in some comfortable apartment ashore. . . .

"Mrs. Slocum sat busily engaged with her little girl at needlework. Her baby boy was fast asleep in his Chinese cradle. An older son was putting his room in order and a second son was sketching. The captain's stateroom is a commodious apartment, furnished with a double berth which one might mistake for a black walnut bedstead; a transom upholstered like a lounge, a library, chairs, carpets, wardrobe and the chronometers. This room is abaft the main cabin which is furnished like a parlor. In this latter apartment are the square piano, center table, sofa, easy chairs and carpets, while on the walls hang several oil paintings.

"In front of the parlor is the dining room, which together with the other rooms, exhibit a neatness of which only a woman's hand is capable. . . .

"The captain's baby is the captain's pride and bears an honored name . . . About the first distinguishable utterance of the child was 'Gar.' General Garfield acknowledged the compliment in

an autograph letter to the child. The letter was read by the father
to it and the child said, 'Gar. . . .' "

Another eye-witness to the captain's splendor was his half-sister
Emma, who had accompanied their father to New York, and then
stayed on board a while with the Slocums. A long lifetime later,
Emma Slocomb (sic) Miller wrote me her recollections of that
visit. "The cabin of the Northern Light was fine. Everything was
there as in a modern apartment. There was a pantry boy, a
Philippino, who took care of the pantry work. Very hot days,
instead of our going out to eat, the boy was sent to the restaurant
on Fulton Street. He would bring back a good supply of food. . . .

"Virginia was most kind to me during the weeks I was with
them. She took me sight-seeing to the historical and art museums,
also bought some nice things for me. They took me to Coney
Island to hear Sousa's band of one hundred pieces. I saw nothing
but happiness between Josh and Virginia. I think there was
nothing else. They seemed perfectly happy. Captain Josh was a
kind, thoughtful and fine man."

On the Northern Light, Virginia taught school for Victor,
B. Aymar, and Jessie. On Sundays, there were Sunday School
lessons. Jessie Slocum Joyce remembered her mother did fancy
work, played the piano, harp, and guitar, and sang. She was a
fine dancer, too. "Mother was a remarkable woman. Not many had
the stamina she had. There are none today would live as she had
to. She lived truly as the Book of Ruth says," Jessie wrote
me. After signing her name, she added a title—"The Captain's
Daughter."

Slocum's scrapbook also played a part in the children's education. Jessie wrote that whenever the captain "saw any item that
interested him or amused him he would get out his penknife
and that bit of news would be pasted in. He used to do a lot of
chuckling over some of them. Father and mother always encour-
aged us in reading any and all books." One of the cabins of the
Northern Light, said Victor, had a library of 500 volumes, and
"with its orderly and well fitted bookcases looked very much like
the study of a literary worker or a college professor."

In spite of finely appointed cabins, life on the Northern Light
was not easy. The responsibility was immense. Danger was ever
present. The Tribune reporter had noted how few American sea-

men could then be found. Young men were going West. On American ships, one found not only roving adventurers, and men seeking to escape the restraints of civilization, but drunkards, vagrants, criminals, and degenerates. By and large, foremast hands were being recruited from the dregs of society. Set against them were officers who were often brutal and tyrannical. Under the circumstances, it took a master of uncommon ability, initiative, and courage to handle a ship. He had to counterbalance the inferiority of a large percentage of his shipmates. Besides navigation and seamanship, he needed to know how to use his fists. Slocum knew. Some ten years later, a newspaperman described him as being "as tough as wrought iron and as lively on his feet as a chicken. His fist is not only big, but has a hard, horny Jim Corbett cast that inspires respect. He is a good shot with the pistol. . . ."

The *Northern Light* set sail in August 1882, with a cargo of oil bound for Yokohama, but soon after leaving New York the rudder was found to be out of order, and the ship put into New London, Connecticut, for repairs. The crew, or part of it, claimed this ended the voyage, and that having been paid in advance, as was the custom, they were entitled to keep their pay. Suddenly mutiny flared. In attempting to seize the ringleader, the chief officer was stabbed and mortally wounded. Virginia sprang to the captain's side. "I saw her covering father with a revolver in each hand during the searching of the crew," B. Aymar said. In response to a signal for help, the Coast Guard steamed out. The wounded man was taken ashore; the mutineer, arrested. The rest of the insurgents were locked up on board the ship.

By the time the *Northern Light* was ready to sail again, Slocum had secured a new mate but not a new crew. A good crew was hard to come by. He kept the old one—an unfortunate decision. The *Northern Light* would sail around the world, and the captain have trouble all the way. On the voyage out to Yokohama, he rescued a party of five native Gilbert Islands missionaries, 600 miles from their home. They had been adrift in an open boat forty days.* "Often and often," he wrote later, "in the hour of

* Slocum's account of the incident, "Rescue of Some Gilbert Islanders," probably written in the middle 1880s, was published by himself as an appendix to the 1890 edition of *Voyage of the Liberdade*.

great distress and bitter sufferings, the story of the Islanders has come to my thoughts, and I have said: 'My state is not yet so bad as theirs, nor my condition so woeful as that of the stricken sailors on the pest-ridden bark, upon the inhospitable coast. . . .' "

After discharging her cargo, and the Gilbert Islanders, in Japan, the *Northern Light* sailed for Manila, where she reloaded with sugar and hemp consigned to Liverpool. Sailing through the Sunda Strait, she passed by the volcanic island Krakatoa, in the Netherlands East Indies, just a few days before it erupted. The eruption, the greatest in modern times, began in May, but the "paroxysmal explosions" did not occur until 26–28 August 1883. Stones, dust and ashes shot up from the volcano to a height of 17 miles or more, then fell on surrounding islands so thick as to bury their forests. The sounds were heard for thousands of miles. Waves fifty feet high were churned up. Nearby coastal and island villages were swamped, 36,000 lives lost, and atmospheric conditions disturbed throughout the world.

The *Northern Light* must have sailed by during the time the volcano was active, but before the final upheaval. B. Aymar wrote me, "Had we been three days later in that region we would have been suffocated by the fumes—something to think of anyhow." As it was, the ship sailed for many days through fields of floating pumice stone, and her decks were covered with ashes.

Trouble continued. As the *Northern Light* neared the Cape of Good Hope, heavy seas twisted her rudderhead off. She also began to leak in the topsides. Water got below and melted the sugar in the lower hold, till the ship became so crank that the hemp stowed in the between decks had to be jettisoned to keep her reasonably upright. Under jury steering gear, she finally made Port Elizabeth. There the cargo was discharged and the ship overhauled. She was laid up two months in the South African port.

Once again, an officer had to be replaced, this time on account of illness. A man named Henry A. Slater, an ex-convict as it turned out, was shipped in his stead. *American Merchant Ships, Series Two* (Salem, Mass., 1931) states that Slater, before signing on, "had arranged with some of the crew to murder Captain Slocum and take possession of the ship." Soon after the ship put to sea, homeward bound, Slater must have tried to start something. Rightfully or wrongfully he was put in irons, imprisoned, and so kept

for 53 days, the balance of the passage to New York. The turbulent
round-the-world voyage of the *Northern Light* had taken a year
and a half, but the last of it had not been heard.

In New York, the trouble between Slocum and Slater continued
in federal court. On Slater's testimony, the captain was convicted
on charges of false and cruel imprisonment. Slocum was fined
$500, which his underwriters paid. Slater also entered a civil suit
for damages, but ended it suddenly, before it could be brought
into court. The *Boston Herald* carried the report:

"New York, Jan. 12, 1884. Henry Arthur Slater called on Mr. B. S.
Osborn, editor of the Nautical Gazette, today, and said he had suffered
all he wanted to, and had had enough. He said that if Mr. Osborn
would hear what he had to say, he would make a clean breast of everything. So Mr. Osborn heard Slater, whose words were taken down in
shorthand and sworn to before the editor, who is also a notary public.
They were in substance as follows: 'I was late second officer on board
the ship Northern Light, of which Joshua Slocum was master. On a
voyage from Port Elizabeth, South Africa, to New York, I was confined
as a prisoner by order of the said Slocum, and I was accordingly put
in irons and confined as above stated. I heard Chief Mate Mitchell tell
Capt. Slocum that I had said I would kill Capt. Slocum and his wife if
I ever got out of irons. I believe that was the reason I was kept so
closely confined. Since I have been at liberty I have found out that
Capt. Slocum ordered me to be brought up on deck every day and that
I should have sufficient food and water every day. Mitchell told Capt.
Slocum that if I was brought up on deck, I would create a mutiny and
murder all the afterguards. I do not blame Capt. Slocum for the treatment I received . . . I never gave my authority to enter a civil suit
against Capt. Slocum and I do not wish the suit to proceed. I now see
that both Capt. Slocum and myself have been made the dupes of the
very men who ought to have protected us, and that the whole affair is
made to get money out of Capt. Slocum, to be distributed among
them . . .'

"'Slater said he came voluntarily,' said Mr. Osborn. 'He said he had
put Slocum in a bad hole, and was in an equally bad hole himself. He
said he did not know what he had been doing. He had signed lots of
papers, but did not know what they were. . . .'"

The aftermath of the voyage of the *Northern Light* hurt Slocum.
He had to defend himself in law suits. While his time was taken

up in this way, another master had to be engaged for the ship. These suits damaged him financially and did not add to his reputation.

As a commander, what sort of reputation had he had? The editor of the *Nautical Gazette,* who took Slater's affidavit, said that Slocum was an "A-1 man, a genuine Yankee captain of high reputation." The *Tribune* reporter described the captain as "one of the most popular commanders sailing out of this port, both on account of his general capability and his kindness to his crew." The marine historian, Frederick C. Matthews, wrote that Slocum, "while a strict disciplinarian, requiring immediate obedience to orders," was also "of a kindly disposition and a fair just man."

Some years later, according to a Boston newspaper, Slocum said of himself, "I'm not a martinet but I have my own ideas of how to run a ship. . . . The old shipmasters treated their crews like intelligent beings, giving them plenty of leeway, but holding them with a strong hand in an emergency. That's my style. . . ."

Not long after the return to New York, a change of ownership was recorded on the ship's register, a document issued by customs authorities. Permanent Register No. 8 issued at New York, 15 July 1882, had listed William Pinckney of New York, Sylvanus Blanchard of Boston, and Joshua Slocum of San Francisco as owners of the *Northern Light.* Slocum was also listed as master but by 24 January 1884 he no longer appeared as either an owner or master. A notation on the register indicates he had sold his shares.

Slocum's shares in the *Northern Light* could hardly have brought him much. The ship needed overhauling but the repair was no longer economically possible. Steam was going ahead; sail was passing. The following year the *Northern Light* was sold to aliens. The ship which had been Slocum's best command was cut down and converted into a coal barge—"ignominiously towed by the nose from port to port," Slocum wrote later.

If Slocum had more than his share of troubles, one of his problems was that he chose to stick with a dying profession. Like the ships they captained, sailing masters were becoming a thing of the past. Never again would Slocum command a ship to compare in size with the *Northern Light.* Never again would he be as prosperous as when he sent for his father. The high point of his merchant marine career had passed. The long descent had begun.

5

a little bark

Changing ships is like changing loves. The old love exits; the new love arrives.

Using the last of the gold pieces he had received for the *Pato*, Slocum bought a sailing ship from Thos. Whittridge in Baltimore; "a little bark which of all man's handiwork seemed . . . the nearest to perfection of beauty, and which in speed, when the wind blew, asked no favors of steamers." A time when masters, as well as owners, were turning to steam, was hardly the moment to invest one's dwindling means in a sailing ship. But Slocum was determined to keep on as he had begun. Like Thoreau, he heard a different drummer, and stepped to the music he heard.

The *Aquidneck*, as the fast sailing bark was called, was hardly a fifth the size of the *Northern Light*, but more like the old *Amethyst*. She had been built in Mystic, Connecticut, in 1865 and so was almost twenty years old. Permanent Register No. 65 issued at Baltimore, Maryland, on 4 March 1884 described her as having one deck, three masts, a round stern and a billet-head, that is, a small scroll used in place of the more ostentatious figurehead. She was 138 feet long, 29 feet wide, 13 feet deep and measured 343 gross tons. Joshua Slocum of Baltimore, formerly of San Francisco, California, was listed as sole owner and master. While the *Aquidneck* went into drydock for needed repairs, Virginia and the children went to live with one and another of Joshua's married sisters settled in the neighborhood of Boston. Like Slocum himself, reversing his forebears' migration, most of his brothers and sisters had left Nova Scotia for the States.

Virginia welcomed the change to a life ashore, for the tumultuous voyage of the *Northern Light*, with its constant alarms, had undermined her health. "Her heart was not strong," her daughter wrote me. Temporary lodging with her sisters-in-law seems to have been congenial. One of them, describing her as "a handsome woman," said that Virginia and the captain "were deeply in love and could be completely oblivious of everyone and everything if they could be together."

Some time in the spring of 1884, the *Aquidneck* was ready to make her first voyage for her new commander and owner. "Victor and I," wrote B. Aymar, "were at Aunt Alice's home when we were ordered to come to Baltimore at once." The ship was loaded with flour for Pernambuco, Brazil, and Slocum, with his family aboard, set sail once more.

Garfield, born too late to remember the *Northern Light,* remembered the later home well. "The saloon on board the *Aquidneck* was a beautiful room," he wrote me, "parquetry floor, doors, paneling, and ceiling painted flat white, open scrollwork over the stateroom doors painted light blue and gold. The captain's room had a full size bed, porthole, etc., and the other rooms a single bunk, a bracket lamp (oil) held by a metal bracket, two metal rings to allow the lamp to remain upright when the ship rolled or pitched. There was a long table and in rough weather racks were put on the table. The table was built around the mizzenmast. Swivel chairs were bolted to the deck around the table. There were also some loose chairs, a skylight with colored glass, a canary that sang all day—a beautiful singer. Also a square grand piano was bolted to the deck. A large lamp was bolted onto the mizzenmast. There were wall bracket lamps, and double doors in the companionways, forward and aft. There was a cabinet with glass doors for carbines, guns and revolvers and ammunition. The pantry was off the saloon. Plates and saucers were kept in boxes on a shelf built the right size, with slots: cups, mugs, soup tureens hung on hooks. There was a store room for groceries, canned goods, etc. for all hands. The deck house was amidships: a fully equipped carpenter shop, galley, staterooms for the bosun, cook and carpenter. On the roof were pens for sheep, pigs and fowl. . . .

"Father had a large library on board the *Aquidneck*. He also bought a lot of books and toys for me. He was very kind and stern. . . ."

Victor described the bark as being "as close to a yacht as a merchantman could be."

It was a pleasant voyage to Pernambuco. While the *Aquidneck* lay moored by the breakwater, Virginia and the children had good times ashore. There was a cocoanut grove where they liked to picnic on Sundays.

From Pernambuco, the Slocums sailed for Buenos Aires, but soon after passing Santa Catarina Island, 500 miles below Rio, Virginia was taken ill. She stopped making candy, doing embroidery, making stockings, and tapestry. "I remember the piece she worked on last," Garfield wrote me. "She left her needle where she stopped." Virginia went to bed and did not see land again. She was in bed when the ship reached the Plata River. At Buenos Aires, the estuary of the Plata is 34 miles wide, but so shallow that in those days, before channels were dredged, ships drawing more than 15 feet were forced to anchor 12 miles outside the city.

Anchored in the outer roads, Slocum went ashore in a public sailboat to interview prospective shippers of freight. He hoped to get a cargo for Sydney, as Virginia wished, so that she could see her people again. Thirteen years had passed since she had married and sailed away. Her parents had not yet laid eyes on her children. Before Joshua disembarked he and Virginia agreed on a signal to call him back to the ship in case he should be needed. The signal was the blue and white flag letter "J"—J, for Joshua.

Early on the morning of 25 July, Virginia was up again, busy salting butter for the voyage which she hoped would take her home. B. Aymar helped her. He was twelve. But soon, Virginia called him to hoist the letter "J" at once.

"Father returned about noon," B. Aymar wrote, "and I was called by father at about 8 p m to kneel at her bedside as she breathed her last—her eyes closed and motionless." Virginia, not yet 35, was dead.* She lies buried in the English cemetery at Buenos Aires.

For the second time Joshua Slocum lost the person closest to

---

* The immediate cause of Virginia's death is not clear. George Walker, her brother, later told B. Aymar that death had come as a result of childbirth, or miscarriage, but the son did not think so. He thought it was her heart. "I never cared to ask father," he wrote me.

him, a woman. Loss and separation experienced when his mother died was re-enacted in the death of his wife. His mother had died young but not as young as Virginia. Joshua wrote in Virginia's Bible:

Family Record

Virginia Albertina Walker
Born Aug 22 1849 New York City
Married 31st January 1871 to Joshua Slocum
Died 25th July 1884
Thy will be done not ours!
Joshua Slocum
Born Feb 20th 1844
Married Virginia A. Walker 31st Jan 1871 at Sydney NSW
Died

"Thy will be done not ours!" Slocum seems to have been on easy conversational terms with his Deity. "Old Sailors may have odd ways of showing their religious feelings," he wrote years later to a cousin in the clergy, "but there are no infidels at sea . . . we old sailors, even, have stowed away in our hearts, and God knows it, the longing to call on a Father and we do so."

B. Aymar, who inherited Virginia's Bible, wrote me that she "knew father better than all others. She knew father could sail ships. She also knew more about father than herself. On many occasions mother had proved herself to be very psychic—and had many times reminded father of failures that need not have occurred had he taken her advice.

"Father learned to understand her powers of intuition and he relied on it fully until she passed on. His ill fortunes gathered rapidly from the time of her death."

Only a few days after Virginia was buried, Slocum ran the *Aquidneck* aground on a sandbar in the Plata. After getting her off at heavy cost, he sailed for Boston with his broken family. B. Aymar was put in charge of both Jessie and Garfield. "The latter (about three) was very stubborn so Jessie helped me." After the voyage home without his mother, B. Aymar never again went to sea "although father wept when I begged to be left ashore at his sisters' in Massachusetts."

To Virginia's mother in Australia, Slocum wrote:

Washington D.C. 10th Feb 1885

Dear Mother

While I (am) here with mine and Virginia's old friends my heart goes out again for your poor aching heart. I have just been to the art galleries looking at the picture that our dear one looked at a year ago And talked with friends high in the society of this great capitol who loved her dearly but who say oh we will soon meet her in Heaven.

I feel most of the time that Virginia is with me and helping me and that her noble soul is helping support her mother . . . and I doubt not at all but that she is with you and me more now than before—It has pained me tho to have to give up my beatiful wife when we wer getting so many enjoyable friends and getting in comfortable circumstances—I would have had some money in ha(n)d by this time if I hadnt got crazy and runn my vessel onshore. As it is now I am just swimming out of trouble on borowd money of cour the vessel is mine and I may be lucky enoght to earn something with he(r) if I do you shall heare from me dear mother, in the meane time George must help you . . . —Victor will write you often he is going with me this time, he is a navigator and I take no mate * except him this time, and a second mate.

The children are just lovely and healthy. I shall strive to do well by my loved ones children I shall try mother to make her Happy in Heaven she was I know happy with me here—she knew that I loved her dearly, and always loved to be in her company—What a terrible separation this has been to me I send you a photo of o(u)r dear ones grave—the name Virginia is in gold and shall be kept in gold as long as I live

Good bye Dear mother We will write you from Brazil . . .

Yours in affliction

/s/ Josh

Acting and thinking now without Virginia, Slocum tried to hold his course. He made three swift voyages between Baltimore and Pernambuco. On one, he carried a cargo of pianos and machinery. In those days, stevedores drove cordwood among the lading, but on this particular voyage, the rolling and pitching of the ship worked the cordwood free. "The pianos got loose. Snapping of wires was heard all over the ship. Father lost money on that cargo," Garfield wrote me.

* Deck officer on a merchant ship.

34

B. Aymar summed up: "Father's days were done with the passing of mother. They were pals. . . ." Garfield put it even more clearly: "When she died, father never recovered. He was like a ship with a broken rudder."

Slocum, in losing Virginia, lost the woman in whom he had found the warmth and companionship a man must find or remain forever hungry.

The *Northern Light*. Peabody Museum of Salem.

The *Aquidneck*, drawn by Charles D. Peirce, 1868 or 1869.

Joshua Slocum, ca. 1883.

Virginia Albertina Walker Slocum, the captain's first wife, in the 1870s.

WIFE OF CAPTAIN JOSHUA SLOCUM
Died 25 July 1884
Aged 35 years

Virginia Slocum's grave, Buenos Aires, 1884.

Joshua Slocum, 1889. Photo by Mathew B. Brady, Washington, D.C.

The *Liberdade*, 1889. Smithsonian Institution.

Slocum, Hettie (his second wife), Garfield, and Victor aboard the *Liberdade*, 1889.

Joshua Slocum, ca. 1890.

The *Destroyer* in Pernambuco Harbor, 1893.

Part II

6

*the voyage
of the "Aquidneck"*

After Virginia's death, Slocum continued freighting between
Baltimore and Pernambuco, Brazil. Victor sailed with him as
mate. B. Aymar, Jessie, and Garfield stayed ashore with relatives.
For a year and a half Slocum went his way "sad and very
much alone, seeking company and a remedy for his lonely life,"
B. Aymar wrote me. Slocum was troubled. In his search for
guidance and help he consulted a spiritualist, not at all an unusual
step in those days.

An analysis of Slocum's handwriting shows "the consistent
repression of a strong sensuousness and a need for actual close-
ness . . . some pasty (sensuous) lines present at all times but
most frequent in the letter of 1885 (the letter to Virginia's
mother). The determined pressure of the downstrokes of letters
. . . bespeaks an extraordinary desire to prove his masculinity
under all circumstances." In other words, the masculine protest,
as the handwriting reveals it, is excessive, and must have origi-
nated in an enormous intensity, or frustration of longing for
feminine warmth. Graphology, as a tool for the study of personal-
ity, is increasingly understood and appreciated.

On a visit to his three younger children who lived with his
sisters Alice and Etta at Natick, Massachusetts, Slocum met a
first cousin who had just come down from Nova Scotia. Her name
was Henrietta Miller Elliott. Hettie, as she was called, had been
born in Annapolis County in 1862, two years after Slocum had
left Nova Scotia and begun his career.

A dressmaker and seamstress, Hettie, 24 years old, is said to have been pretty. Slocum, 42, was lonely. He was "an ardent person, certainly demonstrative in showing affection," a relative wrote me, "and Hettie was no doubt bedazzled by his attentions when he was considered successful." Joshua and Hettie married on 22 February 1886 in Boston. "Her family was not so keen on the marriage on account of Josh wanting his wife with him on the trips," the same relative wrote. But apparently Hettie was game to try the seafaring life. Virginia had been dead nineteen months.

On 28 February, six days after their marriage, Joshua and Hettie were ready to sail. The voyage was destined to be the *Aquidneck's* last, and Slocum's last as a merchant captain.

By the mid-1880s, most sailing ships were tramp ships, that is, vessels not making regular trips between the same ports but rather taking a cargo when and wherever offered, and to any port. Small single-deckers like the *Aquidneck* could find little employment in foreign trade except in carrying mineral oils, mostly between the United States, the West Indies, and South America; or in the coasting business, handling coarse freights such as lumber or coal. The cream of the traffic, and higher rates, went to steamers. Steamers could calculate their time of arrival whereas, as every merchant knew, the time of even the swiftest sailing ship could be extended for weeks by adverse winds.

With Hettie and Victor, fifteen now and serving as mate, and Garfield, five years old, grouped around him, Slocum set sail on a routine job; carrying case oil to Montevideo, Uruguay—kerosene in 5-gallon cans, packed by twos in wooden cases. The "crew mustered ten, all told; twelve had been the complement when freights were good," Slocum wrote later. Undermanned crews were common practice as masters and owners economized. Some of the toughest shipboard conditions prevailed as the age of sail closed down.

Once his crew came on board, Slocum was anxious to get under way. He sailed in spite of predicted storms. The *New York Times*, 1 March 1886, reported a gale blowing off the coast and the temperature down to zero. For the first time in years the North River was frozen over. The following day a hurricane battered the *Aquidneck*. She began to leak and had to be pumped continu-

ously for 36 hours. Riding out the storm, Slocum made Montevideo on 5 May, 66 days after leaving New York.

After discharging the case oil, Slocum did a little freighting
up and down the east coast of South America. While loading
baled alfalfa hay at Rosario, a river port in Argentina, he encountered an epidemic of cholera. His cargo of hay was consigned
to Rio de Janeiro in Brazil but because of the Argentine epidemic,
the Brazilian authorities would not grant him clearance for Rio
but only for the quarantine harbor, Ilha Grande, 60 miles outside
the city.

However, by the time Slocum arrived at Ilha Grande early in
January 1887, all Brazilian ports were closed to vessels coming
from plague-stricken Argentina. As a result, he was not permitted
to unload his cargo even there, at the quarantine harbor, and to
this circumstance Slocum attributed his subsequent troubles and
eventual loss of the *Aquidneck*. As he wrote the following year
to Thomas F. Bayard, Secretary of State, "The nature of my
profession causing often, one adversity to follow one, has made
no exception for me." He would never forget Captain Custodio
de Mello commanding the armored cruiser *Aquidiban,* who turned
him away at gunpoint and, though Slocum begged, would not
allow fresh provisions to be put aboard the *Aquidneck*, an added,
almost personal, injury. What to do with the hay was now the
question. "One person," Slocum wrote later, "suggested that the
case required me to pitch the whole cargo into the sea! This
friend, I may mention, was from Boston." The friend, identified
only as a man, probably gave good advice. It might have been
wise to have followed the Boston Tea Party precedent. Slocum,
however, decided "there was no way but to return where the
cargo came from, at a ruinous loss, too, of time and money." And
so he sailed back to Rosario and lay there with the cargo in,
waiting for quarantine restrictions to lift.

"At last, April 9th, 1887, news came that the Brazilian ports
were open. . . . This made a great stir among the ships. Crews
were picked up here and there, out of the few brothels that had
not been pulled down during the cholera, and out of the street
or from the fields. . . . Mixed among them were many that had
been let out of the prisons all over the country, so that the

scourge should not be increased by over-crowded jails. Of the six who shipped with me," Slocum wrote, "four had been so released from prison, where they had been serving for murder or highway robbery; all this I learned when it was too late." Sailing a second time from Rosario, Slocum arrived 11 May at Rio de Janeiro where he delivered the hay he had loaded six months before. More than a year had passed since he sailed from New York.

From Rio, Slocum turned the *Aquidneck* south, "partly laden," he noted in his journal, "with flour, kerosene, pitch, tar, rosin and wine, three pianos . . . and one steam engine and boiler, all as ballast. . . ." On the way down a storm caught the bark unprepared, threw her on her beam-ends and shook up the non-paying cargo. In due course, however, the pianos, "fearfully out of tune," and the other goods were landed at Antonina, Brazil.

On the night of 23 July 1887, as the bark lay at anchor in Antonina harbor, some of the crew Slocum had shipped at Rosario tried to murder and rob him. Disturbed by the threatening attitude of some of the men earlier in the day, Hettie had been unable to sleep. She heard someone whispering and moving quietly on the deck near the cabin. Alarmed, she wakened Slocum and urged him not to go on deck by the forward companionway. Her advice may well have saved his life. "Nothing," Slocum wrote afterwards, "justifies a visit on the poop deck after working hours except a call to relieve sickness, or for some other emergency, and then secrecy or stealth is non-permissible. . . . Arming myself, therefore, with a stout carbine repeater, with eight ball cartridges in the magazine, I stepped on deck abaft instead of forward, where evidently I had been expected."

As Slocum came on deck, four of the crew were waiting. Greeting him with oaths, they challenged him to order them forward. He did so. The men, instead of obeying, attacked him with knives. Slocum managed to shoot two of his assailants, killing one of them. "It is idle to say what I would or would not have given to have the calamity averted . . . ," he wrote. "A man will defend himself and his family to the last, for life is sweet, after all."

The shooting resulted in Slocum's arrest and detention in Antonina. The *Aquidneck*, meanwhile, loaded a cargo for Montevideo and sailed with a Spanish master in charge, Victor going as mate and also his father's representative. On 23 August, a month after the homicide, Slocum pleading self-defense was acquitted in Municipal Court and released. He was free now to depart. Leaving Hettie and Garfield in Antonina, Slocum hurried by steamer to Montevideo where he rejoined his ship.

Exacerbated by the chain of events, and by lack of satisfaction received by appealing to local authorities, Slocum now wrote the President of the United States. In a long man-to-man letter to Grover Cleveland, Slocum gave a personal account of the treatment he had received at Ilha Grande. He said he was discriminated against. "My Bill of Health," he wrote, "was the same as that of other ships then discharging at Ilha Grand. . . . We had no sickness onboard and we broke no law. We paid the legal fee for . . . documents which should have admitted us but were turned away . . . For this I have prayed to our worthy minister at Rio de Jainearo and also protested before the U.S. Consul. . . . Not having reply to my suplication . . . I come, Sir, with my case to the first man in all the land. I have sustained a ruinous loss through no fault of mine which bids to throw me out of my home afloat."

Hard luck continued to dog the *Aquidneck;* further losses lay ahead. At Montevideo, Slocum dismissed the Spanish master who had brought the bark from Antonina and himself resumed command. The change in master led to a dispute with the crew. To satisfy consular officials, Slocum paid the men off, then rehired them. In the interval between, the men went ashore and became exposed to smallpox. When the *Aquidneck* turned north again, it sailed with an infected crew.

Soon after sailing, smallpox broke out. Following "the most dismal," he said, of all his nights at sea, with his crew either sick or dying, Slocum had to turn back. Victor, the ship's carpenter and the cook, the only three hands able to work, the *Aquidneck*, in Slocum's words "a drifting pest house," limped into Montevideo. There the sick were removed, the ship disinfected, and Slocum relieved of a thousand dollars in costs. Shipping a new crew, Slocum and Victor headed north for Antonina where Hettie and Garfield were waiting.

"Breathing once more the fresh air of the sea," Slocum wrote, "we set all sail. . . . Fine weather prevailed. . . . One day, however, coming to an island . . . we came to a stand, as if it were impossible to go further .. . . . a spell seemed over us. I recognized the place as one that I knew very well; a very dear friend had stood by me on deck, looking at that island, some years before. It was the last land that my friend ever saw. . . ." The island was one of the little places off Santa Catarina, Brazil, and the friend who had stood by him was Virginia. Three and a half years had passed since she died.

Rejoining Hettie and Garfield at Antonina, Slocum plunged into a new line of trade: hardwood timber. Shortly after Christmas 1887 the *Aquidneck,* fully loaded with logs, headed for the Atlantic. Crossing Paranagua Bay, "currents and wind caught her foul" near a sandbar and there, on the coast of Brazil, as Slocum wrote, she "stranded broadside on, where, open to the sea, a strong swell came in that raked her fore and aft for three days, the waves dashing over her groaning hull the while, till at last her back was broke—and why not add heart as well! for she lay now undone." She also lay uninsured, though Slocum did not say so. "When the *Aquidneck* was lost," Garfield wrote me, "then father lost all of his money and our beautiful home."

Sold where she went aground, the wrecked bark brought Slocum about $1,000. After paying off the crew, he had, as he said, "a moiety" left for himself. In this plight he might have applied to the nearest U.S. Consul, one of whose functions is to repatriate distressed mariners, but he had no desire for further dealings with consul generals or ministers; and besides, he had his own ideas for passage back to the States.

7

the voyage
of the "Liberdade"

"When all had been saved from the wreck that was worth saving, or that could be saved, we found ourselves still in the possession of some goods soon to become of great value to us, especially my compass and charts which, though much damaged, were yet serviceable and suggested practical usefulness; and the chronometer being found intact, my course was no longer undecided, my wife and sons agreeing with what I thought best.

"The plan, in a word was this: We could not beg our way, neither would we sit idle among the natives. We found that it would require more courage to remain in the far-off country than to return home in a boat which then we concluded to build and for that purpose."

These paragraphs are from *Voyage of the Liberdade*, Slocum's first book. His career as merchant captain has ended. His legend and odyssey have begun. Henceforth he would be a wanderer.

As noted in earlier chapters, Slocum had built boats before. "Next in attractiveness, after seafaring, came ship-building," he wrote. "I longed to be master in both professions and in a small way, in time, I accomplished my desire." If Slocum was an untaught shipbuilder, he had, in his own way, studied the subject. "From the decks of stout ships in the worst gales I had made calculations as to the size and sort of ship safest for all weather and all seas." Wrecked out of the *Aquidneck*, he had only a poor kit of tools to build with but he had a plan—a plan based on boats he was familiar with, but original too—something between a Cape Ann dory and a Japanese sampan. Using lumber cut by native sawyers, salvaging hardware from the *Aquidneck* and improvising the rest, Slocum built a craft, a double-ender, which he called a canoe. Victor worked alongside his father. Hettie sewed the sails, "and very good sails they were, too," Slocum wrote later. Launched on the day Brazil freed her slaves, Slocum, honoring the event, named the canoe *Liberdade*. The canoe would also provide liberation for him and his family from a foreign shore.

To get around regulations, Slocum fitted the *Liberdade* with a net, and then applied for a license to fish inside or outside the bar.

"How far outside the bar may this carry us?" he asked the port authorities.

"Quien sabe!" came the reply—as he wrote in *Voyage of the Liberdade* and added a parenthetical explanation—"Literally translated, 'Who knows?' but in Spanish or Portuguese used for, 'Nobody knows, or I don't care.'"

After sailing in Paranagua Bay a few days "to temper our feelings to the new craft, and shake things into place," the *Liberdade* crossed the bar and entered the Atlantic. "The old boating trick came back fresh to me," Slocum wrote, "the love of the thing itself gaining on me as the little ship stood out: and my crew with one voice said: 'Go on.'"

The *Liberdade* sped north but after a run of 150 miles, a squall struck, tore her sails to shreds, and drove her into Santos harbor under bare poles. There Slocum, sailor-like, chanced on a friend, a Captain Baker, commanding the mail steamship *Finance*, about to take off for Rio. Baker offered Slocum a tow and Slocum accepted, after handing Hettie and Garfield onto the larger boat. "Hettie and I were on board the steamer," Garfield wrote me, "and we would stand and watch for the *Liberdade* to come up over a huge wave. Father had a lot of nerve, strength, and will power. He steered all day and all night. Victor sat in the fore-peak under a tarpaulin, an ax in his lap to cut the hawser in case the *Liberdade* turned over. Father had a lanyard tied to Victor's wrist. Father would pull on it and Victor responded with a pull. Both were wonderful men—plenty of courage and brains and endurance."

In this manner the *Liberdade* made Rio. Slocum called that leg of the journey "the most exciting boat-ride" of his life. "I was bound not to cut the line that towed us so well," he wrote, "and I knew that Baker wouldn't let it go, for it was his rope." In Rio, Slocum exchanged his fishing license for a Passe Especial with a seal on it "as big as a soup plate." In pursuance of his claim for losses while freighting in the *Aquidneck*, and now for the vessel as well, Slocum called at the U.S. Consulate.

On 23 July 1888, the *Liberdade* sailed from Rio. When the "canoe" encountered a whale who lazily scratched its enormous back on the little keel, Slocum quietly noted that "for broad rippling humor, the whale has no equal." There were experiences with dangerous reefs and treacherous natives, but confidence in "the thin cedar planks between the crew and eternity" grew steadily.

Bearing north, about halfway between Cape St. Roque, the easternmost bump on the map of South America, and the Amazon, Slocum steered too close to land. The *Liberdade* labored among shoals and breakers. From this terribly dangerous situation, Slocum, with admirable seamanship, worked her into deep water. "Then squaring away again, we set what sail the canoe could carry, scudding before it, for the wind was still in our favor, though blowing very hard. Nevertheless the weather seemed fine and pleasant at this stage of our own pleased feelings. Any weather that one's craft can live in, after escaping a lee shore, is pleasant weather. . . ."

Continuing north, approaching the equator, the voyagers saw the constellations of both hemispheres but as they sailed north they "left those of the south at last, with the Southern Cross—most beautiful in all the heavens—to watch over a friend," Slocum wrote in a hidden farewell to Virginia.

The boat Virginia had died on haunted him. "A phantom of the stately *Aquidneck* appeared one night, sweeping by with crowning skysails set, that fairly brushed the stars. No apparition could have affected us more than the sight of this floating beauty . . . gliding swiftly and quietly by. . . ."

Thirty-seven days after first setting sail, the *Liberdade* made Barbados. Thence her course lay through the Caribbean. Eighteen more days and the Slocums made land off the coast of South Carolina. They had sailed 5,500 miles in 55 days. Having had enough of the sea, they now welcomed the chance to sail inland waters. Flying the Brazilian and American flags, they navigated the swamps of North Carolina to Beaufort, moved on to Norfolk, and finally arrived at Washington, D.C., 27 December 1888, in what Slocum called "the best of health," and in a craft which cost "less than a hundred dollars outside of our own labor of building." Concluding his narrative of the voyage, Slocum wrote, ". . . we learned to love the little canoe as well as anything could be loved that is made by hands," and then speaking for himself, "With all its vicissitudes I still love a life on the broad, free ocean, never regretting the choice of my profession."

Within two weeks of stepping ashore in Washington, Slocum paid a visit to the State Department "in relation to the case of the *Aquidneck*," as an assistant secretary put it. Keeping the *Liberdade* moored in the Potomac, the Slocums spent the winter in the capitol. Though the voyage in the 35-foot boat brought Slocum notoriety, it did not improve his prospects. But as somebody in the news he had his picture taken by Mathew B. Brady, the famous photographer of the Civil War.

When spring came in 1889, Slocum, Hettie, Victor and Garfield sailed the *Liberdade* to New York. The *New York World* sent a reporter to the waterfront to interview Hettie. His story, a Sunday feature, appeared in the paper on 19 May 1889.

"Tales of Capt. Slocum and his wonderful small boat, La Libertad (sic), have been told far and wide . . . *The World* wanted to know what the 'Captain's Captain,' Mrs. Slocum, had to say about it, and sent a reporter down to the small boat, bobbing and rolling with every ripple of the tide that flowed around the gray stone walls of the Barge Office, close to which La Liberdad was anchored.

" 'Can you get in?'

"This question was Mrs. Slocum's greeting when her husband introduced the reporter, whom he had just handed on board, and who stood at the entrance to the low, canvas-covered deck-house, the only shelter afforded by the limited accommodations of the boat. The hostess sat in the wee cabin on a plank running the length and raised about three inches from the deck. A sitting posture was the only attitude possible unless one chose to lie down. Mrs. Slocum is a young, strong (some words missing here) full brow; bright hazel eyes, a remarkably well-formed 'nez,' a frank smiling mouth, and a chin expressing both firmness and tenderness, are the features of an oval face which has acquired a rich bronze tint from months of exposure to tropical suns and ocean breezes. Here is the face of a woman who would be capable of the most devoted, intrepid deeds, done in the quietest and most matter-of-fact way, and never voluntarily spoken of afterwards.

"She wore yesterday a dark blue serge yachting dress, with short skirt and blouse waist trimmed with rows of white braid, and a blue straw sailor hat, which she had taken off and was holding in her slender brown hand.

"Mrs. Slocum's voice is low and full-toned, although she says she is from Boston—that region of thin, high-pitched feminine utterance. Her manner is gentle, and she spoke with some reluctance of her voyage.

" 'It is an experience I should not care to repeat, although now that it is mine I feel a certain satisfaction in having gone through it. . . .

" 'Just there'—pointing outside the entrance—'stood two big water casks. Behind them provisions were stowed. There's the stove over which we did our cooking.' It was a small iron pot on three legs, in which a handful of charcoal could be kindled. 'When we reached colder latitudes, in November, we sometimes used it to heat the cabin, letting the gas burn off and then placing it at the entrance.'

" 'Didn't you grow weary and lonely during the long voyage?'

" 'The loneliness came and went early in the voyage. The weariness grew because it was impossible to get any exercise. There was no chance to walk on the narrow deck, and much of the time it was not possible even to stand outside.'

" 'Were you more oppressed by a sense of loneliness when you first embarked?'

" 'Yes. When we left Rio they gave us a great send-off. Capt. Slocum had obtained a permit to all ports duty-free, from the marine office, and also had been granted permission to sail under the flag of Brazil. They thought it a great honor to allow so small a craft to carry their colors. Crowds of people assembled on the quays to see us off and they cheered us wildly. It was very exciting. Then, as the land grew dim in the distance and finally faded from sight, it seemed very desolate on the sea.

" 'In a few days, however, I had learned to like the life on board—I became accustomed to my surroundings, and was not only contented but happy. We had plenty of books when we started, at several ports where we stopped we got more, and the steamship which we spoke * gave us a quantity of magazines. Wherever we touched, the most lively interest was manifested, and when we went ashore we were delightfully entertained. At Porto Rico we lay two days. The United States Consul there invited us to dine and drove us out to his father's plantation, where we had a charming time.'

" 'Are you going on another voyage, Mrs. Slocum?'

" 'Oh, I hope not. I haven't been home in over three years, and this was my wedding journey.'

"Mrs. Slocum said she was going from here to Boston for a visit, adding:

" 'I shall travel by rail. I have had enough sailing to last me for a long time.' "

Having no home of her own, Hettie returned to East Boston to live with a sister. Jessie and Garfield went with her. Victor and B. Aymar were each on his own. "Father did not come to that house," Garfield wrote me. Apparently Hettie had gone back to the relations who had not approved of her marriage in the first place. "After the Aquidneck wreck," a relative wrote me, "and the voyage home in the Liberdade, Hettie found she was not wholly for that life. It was bad all around taking Virginia's place as a wife and trying to do right by the children."

Within a span of five years Slocum had lost his wife, his home, his money and now, at age 45, his profession as well. Slocum could not get another command. B. Aymar wrote me his father "spent much of his time in contacting his former business associates, seeking a lead to something acceptable." But nothing acceptable came along. There were no berths for a captain in sail, particularly for a master with some hard luck in his past.

* To communicate by voice or signal with a vessel passing at sea is to speak it.

8

what was there for an old sailor to do?

After sailing the *Liberdade* to Boston in the summer of 1889, Slocum too went to live with a relative, Naomi Slocombe Gates, his father's sister, who occupied a house at 69 Saratoga Street, East Boston. Unemployed, broke and in debt, he wrote the State Department again; he still held the Brazilian Government liable for the loss of the *Aquidneck*.

In spite of everything going wrong, Slocum was resourceful still. He decided to capitalize on the moment of fame his small-boat voyage had brought him. Slocum was to be the last of a line of New England sea captains who turned their logs into narratives. With time on his hands, he wrote *Voyage of the Liberdade* and, lacking a publisher, had it printed at his own expense. Self-publication is almost always an act of desperation and Slocum was desperate. Ever a trader in any line, he would try selling what he had written.

Voyage of the Liberdade, "Copyrighted 1890 by Captain Joshua Slocum," Press of Robinson & Stephenson, 91 Oliver Street, Boston, has become a collector's item. A copy turns up from time to time; I am thankful to have one. Less than 5 x 7 inches in size, 175 pages of good enough paper and well bound in dark green, it has a genteel Victorian look—determined to keep up appearances though scarcely having the means to do so. Doubtless, the author's edition was small but even so, how did the printer get paid?

To the title page of *Voyage of the Liberdade*, Slocum added, "Description of a Voyage 'Down to the Sea.'" It was, he explained, written with "a hand, alas! that has grasped the sextant more

often than the plane or pen." This was hardly an "apology," as he
called it. It was more a proud boast. And well it might be, for
Voyage of the Liberdade is a narrative of personal experience
simply, directly and sometimes humorously told.

It is not unheard of that a man without formal education should
write well. The voice of authentic folk writing has nothing to
do with schooling. What is remarkable in this instance is that
Slocum's reading did not spoil his writing. He announces early in
Voyage of the Liberdade that he has read Mark Twain's *Life on
the Mississippi*. Though influenced certainly by Mark Twain,
Slocum's style is not imitative. Part of the explanation may be that
no matter what he was doing, he never lost his identity. He never
forgot who he was. He always spoke in a voice entirely his own—
a Yankee skipper and trader accustomed to an exact and pungent
use of words. In setting his course in the new element, he took
no unnecessary chances. His professional instincts were sharp.
What the whaleship was to Melville—his Yale College and his
Harvard—the square-rigged merchantman had been to Slocum.
He saw a connection between navigation and writing.

But in spite of its excellence, the book went widely unread.
Among journals and magazines of the day, only *The Critic* noticed
it. In its issue of 5 July 1890, its young co-editor, Joseph B. Gilder,
wrote an enthusiastic review.* Gilder seems to have been the
first contemporary literary man to discover Slocum. "The merits
of the book . . . are clearly attributable to the author. The thing
has not been 'licked into shape for him,' " he wrote. Gilder appreciated the fact that Slocum had written and published without
benefit of editor. Though *Voyage of the Liberdade* did not sell,
both voyage and book had carried Slocum farther than he could
know. In the wisdom of hindsight they seem to foreshadow the
bigger voyage and book to come.

* A few words about *The Critic:* it was founded in New York in 1881, by
Jeannette Leonard Gilder (1849–1916), and Joseph Benson Gilder (1858–
1936). "Jean and Joe start a paper here next Saturday," their older brother,
Richard Watson Gilder, poet and editor of *The Century Magazine*, wrote. "It
is to be called the Critic. It is a wild thing to do, but they have had . . . lots
of encouragement." (Gilder, Rosamond, *Letters of Richard Watson Gilder*,
Boston, 1916, p. 106.) The magazine, one of the first to invite Walt Whitman to contribute, was also the first to publish Joel Chandler Harris's Uncle
Remus stories outside Harris's home town, Atlanta. Book reviewing, however, was the main business.

For the present, however, Captain Slocum worked at whatever he could get. "One day," he later told a sympathetic newspaperman, "when I was doing a bit of an odd job on a boat and a whole lot of coal and dirt mixed—Cape Horn berries they call the stuff—came down all about my face and neck, I stood up, thought of the difference between my state and when I was master of the Northern Light, and quit the job."

Garfield wrote me long afterward that his father told him he was offered a berth as captain by the White Star Line, but that he refused. "I asked father why. He told me, 'I followed the sea in sailing ships since I was fourteen years old. If I accepted this offer, I would have to get used to steamships, and I do not like steamships." Slocum went to work as a carpenter in the famous McKay shipyards in Boston, but did not stay long. "They asked me if I belonged to any union. Then they wanted to know what church I was a member of. It cost $50 to get into the union and I hadn't the cash. It didn't seem to suffice that I belonged to God's great church that knew no bounds of creed or sect. . . ." Times were hard. A financial panic impended.

Then, on a wintry day in 1892, Slocum, walking the waterfront streets in Boston, wondering whether to try once more for a command, or try again at the shipyard, met a friend, a prosperous, retired whaleman, Captain Eben Pierce. Pierce, 20 years older than Slocum, was the inventor and pioneer manufacturer of the whale bomb lance and gun. When he died in May 1902, age 80, the *Boston Herald* called him "one of the last remaining relics of the old whaling days."

"Come to Fairhaven, and I'll give you a ship," the ex-whaler said to the ex-merchant captain. "But," he added, "she wants some repairs." *

When Slocum arrived there the next day, he found the old whaler had, as he later wrote, "something of a joke" on him. The ship was a derelict hulk—an ancient oyster sloop

* Fairhaven lies on the eastern shore of New Bedford harbor. The two towns, separated by the Acushnet River, are joined by a bridge. Fairhaven, much the smaller of the two, had been one of the New England seaport towns which dominated the whaling industry in its great period. Though its whaling fleet had disappeared by the 1890s, fishing interests were still important. With a population of less than 3,000 persons, Fairhaven had the quiet brooding aspect of a New England port declining into a summer resort.

called *Spray*. She was said to have been 100 years old and for
the past seven had been lying high and dry in a pasture beside
the Acushnet river. Battered by time and rotted by disuse, to
Slocum she appeared "affectionately propped up . . . some distance from salt water." In short, the *Spray*, like Slocum, was on
the beach. A Yankee shipmaster does not wear his heart on his
sleeve, and what the captain felt at this moment, he never described. But the sight of the old boat whose sailing days, like his
own, seemed done for, must have stirred him deeply. The meeting
in the pasture between Slocum and the *Spray* was the beginning
of love. From that hour Slocum and the *Spray* would never be
parted.

The people of Fairhaven were puzzled by Slocum's interest in
the old wreck. "The day I appeared there was a buzz at the gossip
exchange: at last someone had come and was actually at work
on the old *Spray*. 'Breaking her up, I s'pose?' 'No; going to rebuild
her.' Great was the amazement. 'Will it pay?' was the question
which for a year or more I answered by declaring that I would
make it pay," he wrote.

Early in *Sailing Alone Around the World,* Slocum tells how he
rejuvenated the *Spray*. Once started on the work, he seems to have
been in a good state of mind, happier one would guess than at
any time since Virginia died. "The seasons came quickly while I
worked. Hardly were the ribs of the sloop up before apple-trees
were in bloom. Then the daisies and the cherries came soon after.
Close by the place where the old *Spray* had now dissolved rested
the ashes of John Cook, a revered Pilgrim father. So the new
Spray rose from hallowed ground. From the deck of the new craft
I could put out my hand and pick cherries that grew over the
little grave." A nice river situation, and a very unusual shipyard.
The neighborhood was called Poverty Point.

About all that Slocum retained of the sloop was the model, her
original lines—and her name. As he removed the old timbers, he
fitted in new. He had easy recourse to wooded areas nearby when
he needed timber, and to white oak growing in the pasture where
the *Spray* was on the improvised stocks. Perhaps as he worked
with adz or plane Slocum sometimes recalled how at Olongapo
in the Philippines, he had built the steamship hull. That had been
long ago. Or he may have thought of the *Liberdade* built only

five years earlier and which he had recently sailed to Washington, D.C., and presented to the Smithsonian Institution.

Slocum took 13 months to complete the *Spray*. Cash outlay was $553.62. To obtain the money, a real sum in those days, he worked on ships fitting out farther down the river in New Bedford harbor.

During his time in Fairhaven, Slocum lived with the practical joking but apparently good-hearted Eben Pierce. Pierce was a bachelor. B. Aymar told me he visited his father in Fairhaven and inspected the new *Spray* coming to life. Garfield wrote me he liked Captain Pierce very much.

In 1959, the Town of Fairhaven set up a monument and bronze plaque at Poverty Point on the site where Slocum rebuilt the *Spray*. At the dedication, 18 April, I met Alice Charry. The daughter of Captain John Charry, Miss Charry, born in 1869, was 90 when I spoke with her. She had lived next door to Captain Eben Pierce and had watched Slocum working on the *Spray*. "The neighbors thought he had a bee in his bonnet," she said. As Miss Charry remembered him, Slocum had "a pleasant voice." He enjoyed free board at Captain Pierce's, she reminisced, and had a room over the kitchen. Miss Charry said that Hettie, who worked in Boston "in a factory or at tailoring," came to Fairhaven several weekends. Sometimes Slocum would go to Boston.

Came at last the day of launching. The craft of questionable build and almost distressing plainness was pushed into the river without fanfare. In Slocum's eyes, and words, she "sat on the water like a swan." The *Spray*, 36 feet, 9 inches overall, 14 feet, 2 inches wide, and 4 feet, 2 inches deep in the hold, had a gross tonnage just under 13 tons; net tonnage, 9. Rebuilt along her original lines—notably broad in the beam—she was able to ship quite a load.

A "smart New Hampshire spruce" was fitted for a mast. Sails were bent, and the *Spray*, with Captain Slocum and Captain Pierce on board, flew across Buzzards Bay on her shake-down cruise. All went well. Practical people, however, questioned the sanity of the venture. Was this a sensible thing to do—spend time and money restoring an outmoded working boat? Bluntly put, would she pay? How would Slocum cash in?

9

*the voyage
of the "Destroyer"*

Six years had passed since Slocum wrote President Cleveland asking for help and intervention. During all that time Slocum had kept after various government officials about his questionable claim against Brazil until finally, on 9 December 1893, a Department of State spokesman sent him its last word.

Capt. J. Slocum
69 Saratoga Street
E. Boston, Mass.

Sir

I have received your letter of the 27th ultimo concerning your complaint against the Brazilian authorities on account of their refusal to permit the American bark "Aquidneck" of which you were master, to enter the port of Ilha Grande, in January 1887. . . .

The matter was duly called to the attention of Brazilian Government and an investigation requested. From the reply of the Brazilian Government, a copy of which was furnished you some three years ago, it appeared that at the time of your voyage, cholera existed in Rosario . . . that while the Consul at Rosario did grant the necessary clearance papers to the bark "Aquidneck" on Dec. 14th yet, owing to the rapid spread of the epidemic, on December 21st before the vessel had arrived at Ilha Grande, an order was issued prohibiting the admission into Brazilian ports of any vessel with a cargo of forage coming from Argentine ports; that it was in consequence of such order that the authorities of Ilha Grande refused to admit the "Aquidneck."

The Brazilian Government denied any liability for damages occasioned by its action, holding that the preservation of the public health was of greater importance than commercial profits.

It is believed that this Government would in a similar case, adopt the same measures.

This Department therefore, does not feel warranted in taking any further action.

This letter did not reach Slocum; he was on his way to Brazil. On 7 December 1893, two days before it was written, Slocum had set out as "navigator in command" of a warship towed by a seagoing tug.

Two months earlier, Slocum's old adversary, Custodio de Mello, now an admiral, had seized control of naval forces at Rio de Janeiro and demanded the resignation of the President, General Floriano Peixoto. Peixoto had replied by buying abroad whatever warships his agents could find. In the United States they purchased the 130-foot iron gunboat *Destroyer,* a new and untested invention of John Ericsson's.*

This was the vessel Slocum set out on. Though he had not been able to obtain a merchant ship, he was, said a newspaper report, "highly recommended" to Peixoto's agents, perhaps because only four years before he had shown his daring in coming up from Brazil in the canoe *Liberdade.* Daring was required. The *Destroyer* had never put out to sea; her seaworthiness was entirely unknown. Slocum had compelling incentives for undertaking the job. He needed the money. Also, having been thwarted six years in his irrational attempt to collect from Brazil for the wreck of the *Aquidneck*—B. Aymar wrote me his father was asking $50,000 damages—he welcomed the chance to return to Brazil to see what he himself could do about it.

"Frankly it was with a thrill of delight that I joined the service of Brazil to lend a hand to the legal government of a people in whose country I had spent happy days," Slocum wrote in the introduction to his *Voyage of the "Destroyer" from New York to Brazil.* Actually, his concern was even more personal than that.

* John Ericsson (1803–1889), Swedish-born ordnance engineer, had developed the iron-clad warship, *Monitor.* His *Destroyer,* which embodied a submarine torpedo—forerunner of the modern torpedo-boat destroyer—was left on his hands when he died. A long period of peace had kept him from trying it out.

Near the end of his little book he wrote, "Confidentially: I was burning to get a rake at Mello and his *Aquideban*. He it was who in that ship expelled my bark, the *Aquidneck* from Ilha Grand some years ago. . . . I was burning to let him know and palpably feel that this time I had in dynamite instead of hay."

Slocum and de Mello, however, did not meet; nor did the *Destroyer* see action. The *Destroyer* reached Bahia 13 February 1894 after, in Slocum's words, "the hardest voyage that I ever made, without any exception at all." There she was handed over to Brazilian sailors.

The new crew, "bean-eaters from the fields and mountains . . . ," Slocum wrote, "whether from pure cussedness or not . . . stove a great hole in her bottom . . . 'accidentally,' they said." Accidentally or deliberately, when the Brazilians sank the *Destroyer* in Bahia Basin they scuttled also Slocum's prospect of pay. He could not collect. Instead of one grievance against Brazil, he now had two.

Slocum returned north by steamer in March. In Fairhaven, living aboard the sloop, he found an outlet for his frustration. "From the quiet cabin of my home on the *Spray*, the reminiscence of a war." So begins *Voyage of the Destroyer*, Slocum's second book, only 37 pages long, a footnote to history, and to the author's life story. From Slocum's point of view the complex Brazilian internal struggle had been an opéra bouffe war. "The revolt began in Rio . . . the date don't much matter," he wrote. "The funny war so far as the navy was concerned finished of itself in March, 1894. No historian can ever say more."

Slocum published *Voyage of the "Destroyer" from New York to Brazil* in 1894, and as with *Voyage of the Liberdade*, he himself footed the printer's bill. This time, however, a cheap job had to suffice. According to Victor, his father ordered 500 copies printed. In years of searching, I have seen three. Paper and paper binding were so poor that most of the copies must have crumbled to pieces. Slocum did not try to sell it; he gave it away.

He sent a copy "as a Christmas present and no more" to Samuel Pierpont Langley (1834–1906), pioneer researcher in human flight, author, and third secretary of the Smithsonian Institution, to whom he had earlier presented the canoe *Liberdade*. Slocum was pleased when he heard that Langley had put *Voyage of the*

Destroyer in the "museum Library." It must have seemed as though the book would enjoy safekeeping and be preserved for posterity. The fact is, however, the Smithsonian cannot find it.

Slocum also sent a copy to the *Century Magazine* but the editors showed no interest. Five years later, however, when the *Century* was serializing *Sailing Alone Around the World*, Slocum was able to sell *Voyage of the Destroyer* to *McClure's Magazine*. In March 1900, *McClure's* published an abridged version.

The Boston papers were delighted with *Voyage of the Destroyer*, especially the more derisive parts. These appealed to the rising imperialist mood of the day. "It Reads Like a Romance . . . as valuable from an historical as from an amusing standpoint . . . ," said the *Boston Globe*. One of Slocum's *Destroyer* shipmates, however, did not find it funny. Lieutenant Carlos A. Rivers, a British soldier of fortune, claimed Slocum defamed him by writing that he had been whipped in a scuffle with the *Destroyer's* black cook, Big Alec of Salem. A reporter brought word to Slocum that Rivers was challenging him to a duel. Sitting on Long Wharf, disentangling a fishing line, the *Spray* tied up alongside, Slocum showed no emotion, the newsman reported. Instead, he "philosophically remarked: 'There are my wife's feelings to be thought of. I have always been of the opinion that duelists should consult their wives. . . .'

" 'Do you think the Lieutenant is on your track? . . .'

" 'I wouldn't be surprised. He is rapacious, and a fire eater. When he comes for me I shall wrap myself up in the American flag and dare him to do his worst. . . .'

"Pressed with more questions, Capt. Slocum declined positively to name the place, time, and weapons for a duel.

" 'My wife,' he concluded, 'would be disturbed to be left a widow. I am going right out of Boston on a voyage. It is better that I catch fish than fight him. Just say that I am a man with a big fist . . . Good day. . . .' " And so ended the duel.

Though the voyage of the *Destroyer* was a digression from the main current of Slocum's life, it had its uses; laughing in a baffled rage, Slocum tossed off in *Voyage of the Destroyer* hilarious anecdotes, and revealing asides.

"Horrors of war! how, when a lad, I shuddered at your name. I was in my ninth year, hired out on a farm when the thrilling news came to our township of a probable religious war. The four little churches bounding our small world, had always been in a light warfare, but *now* the *Catholics* were coming. . . .

"In those days, when I followed the peaceful pursuit of the plough, or rather a harrow it was, which towed by the old gray mare, that I navigated over the fields, already ploughed, and followed at three dollars a month. I say I shuddered then at the thoughts of war. But now I find myself deliberately putting my hand to documents which in those days nothing could have induced me to sign. At this time of life, after being towed under and over a large portion of two oceans, I sign articles of war! And not withstanding my well-known peaceful disposition, I am expected to fight—in gold braid—to say nothing of the halibut-knife as long as my arm to dangle about the heels of my number elevens. . . .

"The motives of war: two men strive to be 'liberators' of Brazil, another is ambitious to giver her 'a new republic'—charging brokerage for the same—others again are ready to fight for mere lucre. My own frailty I have already confessed."

Quite possibly disgusted with himself for having undertaken a mercenary role, Slocum turned to the one hope and solace left him, the *Spray.*

10

*I spent a season
in my new craft*

Slocum had declared he would make the *Spray* pay. The time had come to match words with action. "I had intended using her as a fishing boat," a Boston newspaperman reported him saying, "and did do a bit of it after she was launched, but, good Lord, I couldn't seem to get any fish and when I went lobstering all I could get was short lobsters and after that I'd get in jail if I kept on so I gave it up." Though in his younger years Slocum had fished successfully in the North Pacific, and in the Okhotsk Sea, fishing on the New England coast in the summer of 1894, he found he "had not the cunning properly to bait a hook."

He probably was not doing much fishing. He was sailing instead, and getting to know his boat. Though the origins of the *Spray* are obscure, the foremost student of the subject, the Australian, Kenneth E. Slack, says in his book *In the Wake of the Spray*, that her type was common among fishing and working boats in many parts of the world. "Strength and simplicity were the essential features," Slack wrote, "and utility of far greater importance than mere fashionable appearance."

If the original *Spray* had been one of a common class, rebuilt by Slocum she had to be unique. He had put her together in his own way. "I spent a season on my new craft," he wrote in *Sailing Alone*, and while he did so he almost lost her. Garfield wrote me he was with his father, "on board the *Spray*, outbound from an inlet on the Maine coast. There was very little wind. Father was steering. As the *Spray* almost passed a ledge on the leeward, the powerful undertow lifted her and dropped her on the ledge. The

waves tried to finish the *Spray*. Some help came quickly to our aid
by land and sea. Father threw a coil of rope to some men on shore.
He tied me under my arm pits, held one end of the rope, and told
me to jump. The men pulled me to high ground. Other men, in
dories, got the *Spray* off, and towed her to a place where father
repaired her bottom."

In addition to fishing, more or less, Slocum tried again to get
money from his first book. In limbo and unsure what to do next,
he arranged with Roberts Brothers, a well-known Boston publishing house, to issue a new edition of *Voyage of the Liberdade*. He
took them the plates of his 1890 edition. Correcting type and adding illustrations cost $100, a sum which was charged to the author.
In September, in time for the Christmas trade, Roberts Brothers
published 1,000 copies in three different bindings; red, yellow,
and blue. Printing costs were 7½ cents a copy; binding, 14 cents
a copy. The book was priced at $1. Ten cents a copy royalty went
to the author. If the entire edition had been sold by bookstores,
Roberts Brothers would have netted about $300 and Slocum re-
covered his $100. Slocum, however, aimed to do better. Accus-
tomed to trading in any line, he planned to take his book on con-
signment and sell it himself. From Pemaquid Beach, Maine, 18
September 1894—he was down east, cruising in the *Spray*—he
wrote his publisher.

Messrs Roberts Brothers

Dear Sirs:

Referring to the book "Voyage of the Liberdade," I believe I would
like to take 500 copies . . .

The rough word spoken of when I was at your office, Sirs I think is
on page 48 in the last line, which for a holiday book tobesure should
not be there even in quotation. Please expunge and slip in some other
word.

I would dearly love to revise the little book throughout.

Have tried to do so but as often as I have tried I have fallen into the
same faults of style: too earnestly in the fight on decks: too gloriously
free in the boat on the broad ocean

Let any one reading the story put himself in my place, if he can,
bringing his family around him, and he will see better, maybe, how it
should be told

The best that may be done I fear will be to let it go as a sailors book. . . .

> Very respectfully
> /s/   Joshua Slocum

Very respectfully—and also very defensively. Slocum was not yet sure of himself as a writer. The "rough word" which bothered him was, in its quotation marks, "busted in the jaw." Roberts Brothers left it in. Evidently it did not offend their literary ear or Victorian sensibility.

Slocum's next letter, datelined Sloop Spray, 7 October 1894, came from Gloucester, Massachusetts.

Messrs Roberts Brothers   Boston

Dear Sirs   The little book reached me last evening, forwarded from E Boston.

I think its mak-up very neat and modest, with altogather, a charming appearance.

A thousand thanks for the paines taken with the corrections.

The new illustrations, I think, are particularly good. The negro baby —no beauty tobesure—about whom nothing is said, the reader of the book will I hope always bear in mind, is thrown in free.

Some illustrations from Brazil . . . may come too late. . . . Things move slower in Brazil than in Boston.

I will be in and out of Gloucester. . . .

> Very respectfully
> /s/   Joshua Slocum

On 23 October, still in Gloucester, Slocum wrote again from the *Spray*.

Messrs Roberts Brothers
    Boston

I send along the enclosed sketch as the best I can get from *my* artist: Hard to get the green-horns into the way of sketching breakers! Too much white-water across the deck

The sails set well and she is on the right tack. It may serve as a hint, if not too late

Again, if not too late for correction: Page 86 second line should read: made a mistake, instead of: *were mistaken*

I don't know how to apologize sufficiently for the stupidity of my undisciplined head. Baring the above break of grammar I dont see that one part of the story is much better or worse than the other, in the telling.

Very respectfully
/s/   Joshua Slocum

The new edition of *Voyage of the Liberdade* moved very slowly. When, in 1898, Roberts Brothers sold out to Little, Brown & Company, copies of *Voyage of the Liberdade* were still in stock. Today it is a scarce book.

In his efforts to make a livelihood with the *Spray*, Slocum also tried taking out fishing parties. Garfield wrote me, "Father had a party out sailing, men and women all from Roberts Brothers. We anchored off two lighthouses off Boston harbor. Some fished. One man put up 50 cents prize money for the person catching the first fish. I caught the first fish but was not able to pull him in. A man standing next to me did it for me. The fish weighed 12 pounds, a codfish. Father made a fish chowder. Everybody said it was delicious. Some of the men brought bottles of liquid refreshment which we tied on a line and lowered over the side to cool. Everyone enjoyed the outing."

But neither fishing, book-peddling, nor party sailing solved the problem.

11

resolved on a voyage around the world

There is no way to recreate a figure from the past. Document as much as you can and describe; speculate and ask all manner of question; you still cannot fully explain a given individual.

Nobody knows when or how Slocum got the notion of sailing around the world alone. "I was born in the breezes, and I had studied the sea as perhaps few men have studied it, neglecting all else," he wrote. Fascinated by the sea from the first, Slocum had aspired to, and achieved a conventional sea captain's career. Yet somehow, perhaps through his gift for "neglecting all else," his experience proved, by and large, reductive. By 1894 his life had become simplified. He was down to the *Spray* and his own deeper genius.

Slocum wrote, "I had resolved on a voyage around the world . . . ," a desperate middle-aged resolution. That was as much as he said concerning motivation. Was there something he wanted to sail away to? Something he wanted to sail away from? If sailing no longer served a practical purpose, it still provided a perfect illusion of purpose. There was a job to be done whether it paid or not. Command of a vessel, duty to the ship, the necessity for making decisions, and attending to the business in hand left no room for doubt or regret.

When Slocum first went to work on the *Spray* he had had the open sea in mind. "In rebuilding timber by timber and plank by plank, I added to her freeboard twelve inches amidships, eighteen inches forward, and fourteen inches aft, thereby increasing her sheer, and making her, I thought, a better deepwater ship," he wrote in *Sailing Alone Around the World*. Slocum believed the *Spray* had originally served as an oyster boat on the Delaware coast. Though the type had been a popular working vessel, as a yacht it was quite unheard of. Yet it did make a yacht, and a homey one. The *Spray's* long clean lines and shallow hull gave her a barge-like appearance. She was bluff-bowed and, as already noted, beamy, and had plenty of room on deck. Her one graceful touch was the forepart of her bow, the cutwater.

For some time now the *Spray* had been home to Slocum—he had no other. Presumably, she was comfortable in her way. Forward, was a small forecastle with a couple of bunks; aft, a larger cabin under a low house. Slocum slept in the cabin; cooked, ate, read, and sewed there as well. He also kept a cookstove on deck. J. Duncan Spaeth (1868–1954), professor of English at Princeton University, visited Slocum around 1900 and went aboard the *Spray*. Spaeth wrote me of the cabin "lined with books . . . the cozy and liveable atmosphere, not like a 'yacht' at all, but more like that of the master of an old-fashioned, full-rigged ship." The wheel was only a step or two abaft the companionway. Though the bulwarks were low, "a stout, hard pine rail with stanchions," according to a contemporary account, provided a hold for hands and support in a seaway.

The rig of the *Spray* at that time was the ordinary one of a sloop with mainsail and jib. A short topmast was carried for signaling. She was a very big boat for one man to handle. Garfield wrote me that when he and his father hoisted the mainsail, he would take the peak halyards, while the captain took the throat halyards. "It was a job for two people. The mainsail and gaff were heavy. I know it was hard for him to raise it when he was alone." The sheets were, of course, belayed aft.

Since Slocum's time, admiring yachtsmen have built copies *
of the *Spray* even though the vessel was never designed in the first place to be a yacht. In the early 1950s, at Edgartown, Massachusetts, I went aboard a copy called the Oxford *Spray*, built at Oxford, Maryland in 1929 for R. D. Culler. The Oxford *Spray* had recently been sold and the new owner had added a few improvements Slocum had managed without: a diesel engine

* *In the Wake of the Spray* by Kenneth E. Slack (Rutgers University Press, 1966), records the histories of a couple of dozen of them.

and fuel tanks, a 1500-watt generator, electric lights and heating system, Monel metal water tanks, hot and cold running water and shower, chrome folding lavatory, hand, and also electric toilet, electric refrigerator, gas range, radio direction finder, radio-telephone, depth sounder, photo-electric pilot, Edson steering gear, electric windlass, remote control fire extinguishing system, and a paid hand to help run the boat.

Of "labor-saving appliances" on the *Spray*, Slocum wrote, "there were none." Nor were there any time-saving devices. He had time. It was really quite simple; the age of convenience had not yet arrived. Slocum relied on himself, on the boat he had made, and on "the buoyancy of His hand who made all the worlds."

Slocum had circled the globe five times, but preparations for a voyage alone were something to think about. It had never been done. There was no pattern to follow.

Slocum began getting ready in earnest. One of the first things he thought of was books. He wrote Eugene Hardy, general manager of Roberts Brothers, an undated letter.

Dear Mr. Hardy: If you could let me have the books you so kindly spoke of the other day, when I was at your office, it would be a great help to me I am sure for I shall have some time to read and shall require all that I can get in that direction for recreation. Mr. Wagnalls (old acquaintance) of the house of Funk and Wagnalls told me the other day that he would also put me up some. I may be able to pay for all this kindness at some future time but not now.

A "shop-worn" book would be as good for me as any: so far as the outside goes. . . .

The books came, and on 9 January 1895, Slocum, sounding more like a professor of literature than a deep-water sailor, acknowledged them.

Dear Mr. Hardy:

The handsome pkg. of books from Messrs Roberts Brothers for the Spray library is greatly appreciated. I will be very glad to take the Liberdades (50) on the terms mentioned. . . .

I am completely fascinated with the new books: with Mr. Stephensons but above all with this new book: Life and Adventures of John

Gladwin Jebb by his Widdow. In this case at least, I think The "Wid-
dows mite" a Sovereign Coin to all of us: I think that Thackeray Gold-
smith or even Washington Irving might have written this charming
book. It carries me back to Vanity Fair, Vicar of Wakefield, to Astoria
and even to Granada: "*Quien Sabe* there was no time to bury the dead
in those days" Mr. Jebb will be along with me on the voyage:

A thousand thanks
/s/   Joshua Slocum

Roberts Brothers' latest publication, *A Strange Career*—life and
adventures of J. G. Jebb by his widow, with an introduction by
H. Rider Haggard, meant something to Slocum. "Rarely if ever .
in this nineteenth century," Haggard wrote of Jebb, "has a man
lived so strange and varied an existence. . . . From the time that
he came to manhood he was a wanderer, and how it chanced
that he survived the many perils of his daily life is nothing less
than a mystery. In the end, however, they brought his fate upon
him prematurely. . . ."

Slocum was enchanted by the wife's account of the adventurous,
athletic, sanguine, and gullible husband. It is not hard to see why
this history of riches to rags aroused in Slocum, at that particular
moment, more fellow-feeling than literary acuteness.

"Mr. Stephensons" book (or books) was probably a reference
to Robert Louis Stevenson. Roberts Brothers had several Stevenson
titles on their list, and at least one, *An Inland Voyage,* accompanied Slocum.

According to the *Boston Herald,* Slocum's seagoing library
included Darwin's *The Descent of Man* and *The Expression of
the Emotions in Man and Animals,* Simon Newcomb's *Popular
Astronomy,* Todd's *Total Eclipses of the Sun*—perhaps meaning
David Peck Todd's report on the total solar eclipse of 1878—Henry
Walter Bates's *The Naturalist on the River Amazons,* Macaulay's
History of England, Trevelyan's *Life of Macaulay,* Washington
Irving's *Life of Columbus,* Boswell's *Johnson, Don Quixote, Life
on the Mississippi,* as well as one or more volumes by Robert
Louis Stevenson, a set of Shakespeare, and in the "poet's corner,"
as Slocum called some part of the cabin, the poetry of Lamb,
Moore, Burns, Tennyson and Longfellow.

Since he could not speak of his inner personal motives, Slocum

told instead of his outer conventional one. The purpose of the voyage was to make money by writing travel letters. To his responsibilities as navigator, captain, and crew, he planned to add those of correspondent. It was not a new idea. Two of Slocum's favorite authors, Mark Twain and Stevenson, had done it. Newspaper-sponsored accounts of travel were popular in the 1890s. With the help of Eugene Hardy—Roberts Brothers agreed to act as his agent—Slocum began getting up a newspaper syndicate. "My Syndicade is filling up," he wrote Hardy. "This morning I got the great Mr. Watterson: The Louisville Courier Journal." *
What the *Courier Journal's* managing editor had in fact written was, "I cannot contract with you for the whole of your series of letters. . . . I shall be glad if consistent with your arrangements to have you submit the letters to us, we to pay for what is used."

Slocum had still another idea. Though the *Spray* was one thirtieth the size of the *Aquidneck,* he nevertheless meant to do some freighting and trading. "I shan't carry much cargo," he said, according to a *Boston Globe* reporter, "but the Spray will be pretty well filled with curios of various kinds before she gets back."

From his earlier voyages as a merchant captain Slocum had his charts, compass, sextant, rifles, revolvers, and medicines. Well-wishers and sympathizers in Boston supplied most of the rather primitive equipment he carried, and much of the necessary stores. He was furnished with the latest Massey patent taffrail log for measuring speed and distance.

In the midst of preparations Slocum spoke to reporters who came down to the dock on the East Boston side of the harbor where the *Spray* was moored. ". . . after a talk with the captain and an examination of his boat something of his own confidence communicates itself to the inquirer, and the adventure does not seem so strange or so impossible of successful issue as many less promising ones which have had a happy termination."

A reporter asked the captain how he would handle the boat. "She is very easily managed, even in a breeze," Slocum replied, "and then, too, I have a steering gear which will act automatically

* Henry Watterson (1840–1921), editor and statesman. His editorials in the *Louisville Courier Journal,* which began its existence in 1868, won national recognition.

when the boat is once laid on her course, and that will give me some chance to rest."

What about sleep? Slocum answered that he was used to going without sleep for two or three days at a time. Actually he had not only unusual muscular strength, but exceptional powers of resisting fatigue. Thirty hours at the wheel, in a storm, he later found, did not overtax his "human endurance." But his plan in ordinary weather was to "sleep in the day time and keep the boat going at night. . . . When it blows too hard I shall get out my sea anchor, batten everything down tight, and go below for a sleep and let the gale blow itself out."

Another anonymous reporter quoted Slocum as saying, "I don't go out like the dumb and blind. Understanding nautical astronomy, I will, of course, navigate the world around with some degree of precision natural to any first-rate navigator. But there is one thing new in my outfit, already tested, the workings of which you will hear of in my letters. . . . It will be of great value at sea. . . . Without it I could hardly dare to go on a voyage alone." The captain said he reckoned it would be his last voyage. He said he hoped to make enough out of it to return home to his wife and four children, buy a little farm, and settle down.

Did he really plan to settle down with Hettie some day, or was this merely a traditional speech as he was about to leave for an indefinite time?

Slocum told reporters he would sail alone "unless my wife changes her mind about staying ashore." But he must have known very well that she was not going. He had asked her, and she had replied: "Joshua, I've had a v'yage." She was thinking of the hardships of the trip in the *Liberdade* six years before.

Captain Joshua Slocum, former freighter and trader, and presently little-known author, was ready to put to sea. He described the route he proposed to follow. It bore little resemblance to the one he took. He said he thought the voyage would require two years. His estimate proved conservative by 14 months.

At the very last minute, he was visited by a lady of literary tastes, Mabel Wagnalls, the unmarried 24-year-old daughter of Adam Willis Wagnalls (1843–1924) of the dictionary publishing firm of Funk & Wagnalls. Mabel had been raised with money, music, and books, and wanted to be a writer. The enterprise the old knight of action was about to embark on touched her imagination and heart. Her father had already sent a box of books as a bon voyage present. Now she brought Slocum a little book she had written, 63 pages, *Miserere,* "a musical story." On her visiting card which she pasted inside the cover she wrote, "Wishing you a safe and successful return," a conventional phrase, yet understanding and affection can live in such words.

Slocum had failed in the eyes of the world, and perhaps in Hettie's, but not in Mabel's. The young lady said to the grizzling seafarer, "The Spray will come back."

Cover of paperbound book published by Slocum, 1894.

VOYAGE
OF THE
LIBERDADE

Captain Joshua Slocum

Roberts Brothers edition, Boston, 1894.

First edition, The Century Company, New York, 1900.

SLOOP SPRAY
SOUVENIR

1895 — 1898
U. S. TO U. S.

Pamphlet published and sold by Slocum, 1901.

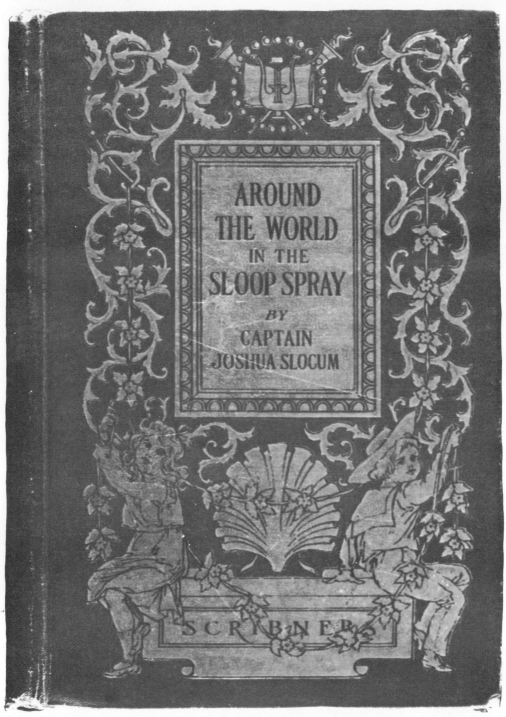

AROUND
THE WORLD
IN THE
SLOOP SPRAY
BY
CAPTAIN
JOSHUA SLOCUM

SCRIBNER

"A Geographical Reader," Scribner's, New York, 1903.

Sloop Spray
Gloucester Mass Oct 7th 1894

Messrs Roberts Brothers
Boston

Dear Sir: the little book reached me last evening, forwarded from Boston.

I think its make-up very neat and modest, withal altogether, a charming appearance.

A thousand thanks for the pains taken with the correction the new illustration, I think are particularly good. The negro baby — no beauty however — about whom nothing is said, the reader of the book will always bear in mind, is thrown in free.

Some illustrations from Brazil I have heard from at New York they may come too late. I was in hopes to get in at least, the one of Pernambuco Recife things were slower in Brazil than in Boston. I will be in and out Gloucester for a couple of weeks

Very respectfully
Joshua Slocum

Letter to Roberts Brothers, 1894.

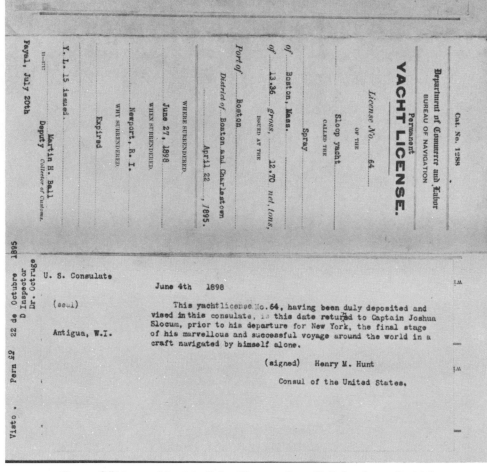

United States Consulate

Cape Town, Cape Colony, Africa

March 23, 1898.

This yacht license, No. 64, after having been deposited by Captain Joshua Slocum
(of the yacht "Spray",) with me at this consulate, on December 30, 1897, is this
day returned to him as he is about to depart for the United States, on his return from
his trip around the world. We shall all miss his genial presence after his departure.

(signed) Frank Willard Roberts
Consul of the United States of America,
at Cape Town,

(Seal)

(St. Bede's Lodge, Three Anchor Bay, Cape Town)

Cat. No. 1288

Department of Commerce and Labor

BUREAU OF NAVIGATION

Permanent

YACHT LICENSE.

License No. 64

OF THE

Sloop yacht

CALLED THE

Spray

of Boston, Mass.

of 13.36 gross, 12.70 net, tons,

ISSUED AT THE

Port of Boston

District of Boston and Charlestown

April 22 , 1895.

WHERE SURRENDERED.

WHEN SURRENDERED.

June 27, 1898

Newport, R. I.

WHY SURRENDERED.

Expired

Y. L. 15 issued.

Martin H. Ball
Deputy Collector of Customs.

Fayal, July 20th

U. S. Consulate

June 4th   1898

(seal)

Antigua, W.I.

This yacht license No. 64, having been duly deposited and
vised in this consulate, is this date returned to Captain Joshua
Slocum, prior to his departure for New York, the final stage
of his marvellous and successful voyage around the world in a
craft navigated by himself alone.

(signed)   Henry M. Hunt

Consul of the United States.

Vista . Perm 42 22 de Octubre 1895 D Inspector Ofricio

Copy of "License No. 64 of the Sloop yacht called the Spray," 1895.

2/

The Spray tis is a palm-tree 2

Keeling-Cocos Islands
Aug 20th 1897

Dear Mr Gilder:— Perhaps you
did not expect to get a letter
from this little kingdom in
the sea; but one never knows
what may happen and the
next mail — mission the had

Keeling-Cocos is a strange
little island owned by the
first settlers, a family of
Scotch of the name of
Clunies-Ross. Nanny things
here are the reverse of other
lands and the women, to
use a homely phrase, rule
the roost. It comes hard
on the men. It would
do the soul of the unsettled
Tuegan woman good to see the
Keeling Cocos and master "Tif a elegant tree

I am looking over these things
as I sail along. The heart
of a missionary is all on
fire to recontruct the religion
of this people of ever one
who frets on his peaceful
land, I hope he will not
be of the soul-destroying
sort that spoiled my
earlier days —

The Clunies-Ross with
myself, men, then comes to
mind, about her thoughts at
sea; while I may ink their
clear — I certainly clean at
sea — than in a busy city
and the thing went on my
mind, that tis the business to
hand, the reckoning, as I
sailed along has been letter
kept than ever before on any
ship of mine ever well off sail

Extract from a letter to Joseph B. Gilder, 1897.

c/o W. S. Hotel, Fulton St, New York City
will reach the undersigned "skipper"
Ans. Sept. 25/99 YACHT "SPRAY," New York
Sept 20th 1899
[Round the world Yacht]

Dear professor Mason :—
    Your note to Century editor
is handed to me
    I need hardly say that I was
delighted, to hear from the Smithsonian
and to hear that you still have the
old Liberdade. Will you give the dear
old craft a slap on her quarter for me?

    And oblige most
        Sincerely Yours
            Joshua Slocum

Otis Tufton Mason (1838–1908) b.
Eastport, Maine

Letter to Otis Tufton Mason, 1899.

E Boston Feb 18th 1900

Dear Mr Buel:

I find my memory still bad on figures. I don't whether the reading you have corrected is 36 ft 9ins or 37 ft 9in anyhow you have it all OK

The depth of hold corrected is four feet two inches not four inches

I would like to say, that if practicable to change a leaf in the edition, I would be only too glad to pay for the trouble and expense of tipping in the corrected one. Anything to keep out of the hands of Butterfly sailors

Yours truly Joshua Slocum

Letter to Clarence Clough Buel, 1900.

11 & 17th St New York N/Y
Feb 27th 1901

Dear Professor Mason,

I am sending by this post, a book of some account, it is a very short one. I am not that that old friend. And I am not for old sins we are no better unless we are helping that I am helping Professor Langley as Professor while we are still Involved out have become sleet a successful flying ship before this had that I could have a second rates position in it, if it were—

I feet sure that when you have time to see anything from story you will find that I consider the human mind above all else that we know it in this respect. You will see that at any rate I could trust even my own human head to find my way about independent of the machine we call Chronometer. I sailed scientifically so, I was in touch with nature as few have ever been. I was aware of it all the time and had never a doubt of the outcome a of my voyage

with great respect
Joshua Slocum

Letter to Otis Tufton Mason, 1901.

Dear Mr Johnson

I have just received a letter from Mr Armstrong saying Wednesday 28th Hadley — all right —

I will be there dangers of the road excepted

with thanks.

I am yours truly

Joshua Slocum

P.S. I see "Good Cooking by" — up in all the Elevated cars. I often wondered, when a boy, if I would become famous and see my name on soap advertisement — But this, the real thing, is better still J. S.

Letter to Clifton Johnson, 1903.

89

West Tisbury, Mass. March 18th 1904

My dear Mr Tripp:

I hope you will pardon my seeming neglect:

I became so interested in trying to keep warm these winter days that I forgot all, except the woodpile

I have an oak grove, fortunately, near my house.

You may send me $1.50 for the book, if you will have it that way.

I make no charge for the anchor. Yours very truly

Joshua Slocum

Letter to William Tripp, 1904.

IN REPLY REFER TO

File No. 53003-n

Department of Commerce and Labor
BUREAU OF NAVIGATION
Washington

March 11, 1910.

Capt. Joshua Slocum,

    Care Century Publishing Company,

    New York City.

Dear Sir:

    I have just finished reading your remarkable volume "Sailing Alone Around the World," in the yacht SPRAY. I enclose from our records a copy of your yacht license, the original of which is now filed in the records of the Bureau of Navigation.

    I enclose a copy of a letter I am sending to the Chairman of the Committee on Government Exhibits at the coming Ohio Valley Exposition.

    Respectfully,

          E. T. Chamberlain
          Commissioner.

B

2 enclosures

The letter Slocum never received, 1910.

"Returned not here supposed lost at sea," 1910.

IN HONOR OF
CAPTAIN JOSHUA SLOCUM

SPRAY

THE FIRST MAN TO SAIL AROUND THE WORLD ALONE
1895 • SLOOP SPRAY 37 FEET 9 TONS • 1898
The Spray was launched near this site and returned
here after her voyage
This plaque given by the citizens of Fairhaven in 1958.

Plaque dedicated at Poverty Point, Fairhaven, Mass., April 1959.

Part III

12

where away
and why alone

The moment arrived when the pieces of life seemed ready to fall into place. "To Go Round the World," the *Boston Globe* announced. "Capt. Slocum Starts from East Boston Alone in His 40-Foot Spray."

A reporter who went down to see him off described him as lively, "a kinky salt," 5 feet 9½ inches tall, weighing 146 pounds, "spry as a kitten and nimble as a monkey." In an eleventh-hour decision Slocum had changed the *Spray's* hailing port from Fairhaven to Boston. He thought the latter would be a better-known name but whalemen had carried the name of Fairhaven to the far corners of the earth. Several times on his voyage around he was asked if Boston were near Fairhaven. "Spray Boston" read the lettering on the *Spray's* stern. As to the course she would take, Slocum appeared uncertain.

" 'Where I shall next be heard from I cannot tell,' he told a reporter. 'I shall make right out to the southward, and when I get among the flying fish it will depend on how I feel how soon I leave them.'

" 'Courage still good?'

" 'Just as good as ever,' was the hearty reply, as the captain cleared away everything forward and prepared to hoist the jib.

" 'Good luck to you then . . .'

" 'Aye, aye' was the cheery response, and the captain sprang aft to the wheel. As the whistles were sounding noon, he sailed away . . ."

Slocum was 51 years old when amid modest fanfare he set sail 24 April 1895. "A thrilling pulse beat high in me," he wrote in

Sailing Alone Around the World. "My step was light on deck in the crisp air. I felt that there could be no turning back, and that I was engaging in an adventure the meaning of which I thoroughly understood. I had taken little advice from anyone, for I had a right to my own opinions in matters pertaining to the sea."

The dramatic exit notwithstanding, Slocum sailed not southward, but eastward, and only as far as Gloucester, twenty miles away. "Waves dancing joyously across Massachusetts Bay" met the *Spray* coming out of the harbor. "Every particle of water thrown into the air became a gem, and the *Spray*, bounding ahead, snatched necklace after necklace from the sea, and as often threw them away." He wanted to put into Gloucester to procure some fishermen's stores, a fisherman's lantern, a gaff, and a dipnet. But even more he needed "again to weigh the voyage, and my feelings, and all that."

The *Spray*, well advertised by the papers, attracted a crowd of the curious and friendly. The captain was given "many useful articles to add to his comfort while at sea. . . . Messrs Wonson and Tarr gave him a supply of copper paint . . ." A Boston lady sent the price of a large two-burner lamp, which the captain thereupon purchased. He used it as a stove by day, as well as a lamp by night.

At Gloucester, Slocum checked out the sloop once more. He worked hard applying two coats of the copper paint to prevent fouling of the *Spray's* bottom. He also picked up a castaway dory, cut it in two athwartships, and by boarding up the cut-off end made himself a boat to take along. Half a dory was about all one man could hoist, and all there was room for on deck. It also served as a tub for laundry or bath.

Slocum spoke freely to newsmen about his plans, but his plans were loose indeed. He had settled on almost nothing including whether he wanted to be alone throughout the entire voyage. That decision, however arrived at, must have come later. He said he had hoped to have the sloop hauled across the Panamanian isthmus, but the railroad's agents had written that it couldn't be done. He was not fazed. He said he would continue down the South American coast instead, perhaps pick up an English-speaking companion at Pernambuco, if one could be found, and then go through the Strait of Magellan. He said he would then cross the Pacific to Japan; from there, go down through the South China Sea and across the Indian Ocean. Entering the Red Sea, he would proceed via the Suez Canal to the Mediterranean and Gibraltar. Finally, by crossing the Atlantic, he hoped to make Boston and home.

Slocum remained two weeks in Gloucester. The delay annoyed his syndicate. Having announced his departure, the papers wanted action, and speed; but speed was not a consideration with Slocum. He left Gloucester in his own time and at his convenience. ". . . as the *Spray* stood out of the cove . . . the front of a tall factory was a flutter of hankerchiefs and caps. Pretty faces peered out of the windows. . . . Some hailed me to know where away and why alone. Why? When I made as if to stand in, a hundred pairs of arms reached out, and said come, but the shore was dangerous." As he sailed eastward he "sat and considered the matter all over again." Again, he asked himself "whether it were best to sail beyond the ledge and rocks at all." Eastward and not southward—as though ineluctably drawn to the land of his birth which he had not seen in many years. As he neared Brier Island whence he had run away to sea almost 35 years before, he asked the way of a fisherman and was given wrong directions. Sailing "through the worst tide-race in the Bay of Fundy," he arrived at the old familiar village where he examined the seams of the *Spray*. He was double-checking. Slocum then wrote a letter to Roberts Brothers, datelined The *Spray*, Westport, N.S., 13 May 1895.

Fetched Westport Friday night. Experienced no difficulties in getting along alone; an no inconveniences I like the novelty of being "alone" even better than I anticipated. I find that I [have] friends, even here, at Westport—"The Island of Plenty" . . .

Will you please give me some hint of how much the first of my experience was disliked if the worst is known? . . .

I will as I get along, I think, make it interesting anyhow I shall try— But I have been put to my wit end to get started right

Do please be patient with me and you will find in the end that I shall try to be fully square . . .

Yours truly
/s/ Josh Slocum

The voyage and the writing were off to a slow start. From the syndicate's point of view, the trip was not going right. On 21 May, almost a month out of Boston and still at Westport, Nova Scotia, Slocum wrote again, this time addressing Eugene Hardy. His spelling, worse than usual, undoubtedly reflected an upset state of mind. Apparently his first reports had not been wholly believed; that would be upsetting indeed.

Dear Mr. Hardy: All very well for Mr. R. to say that; but Mr. H knows how it is himself!

I am in a grand good place to repair my vessel and do it cheaply. Giving her a great going over!

Will sail on the next full tides (full moon)

I think Pernambuco will be my first land-fall, leaving this Thence touching the principal ports on S.A. coast on through Magellan Straits where I hope to be in November. So many courses to be taken after that. I can onlly then go as sircumstances and my feelings dictate

My mind is deffinately fixed on one thing and that is to go round, go with care and judgement and speak of what I see

There's not a reporter here to twist one, that I know of It is a haven of rest, but I shall do my work and sail as quickly as possible.

I guess it would bother my friends to proove that things don't happen on this voyoage just as I relate them.

Thanking you Sir for your kind note . . .

Another month passed and Slocum, still in Nova Scotia, had no more than edged nearer the ocean. At Yarmouth, 20 June 1895, he wrote Roberts Brothers a two-part letter; first, an explanation of the delay, and second, a new plan for getting on with the voyage.

Dear Sirs I arrived here yesterday with the Spray all in good order after having caulked her all over and recruited myself. I had an attack of malaria at Gloucester, from working at the Sloop on the beach there in a sickning ooze. So I had to leave there with the work unfinish, and bide my time. That explaines my slow movements . . .

The letter goes on to say he had changed his mind. He would not head south after all, but instead, sail east.

After all deliberations and careful study of rout and the seasons, I think my best way is via the Suez Canal, down the Read Sea and along the Coasts of India, in the winter months, calling at Aden and at Ceylon and Singapore taking the S. W. Monsoon next summer up the China Sea, calling at Hong Kong and other treaty ports in China thence to Japan and on to California From California I believe I shall cross the Isthmus of Panama The freight agent of the Panama road wrote me that I could not get over the isthmus—we'll see! . . .

My health is excellent now. I experience no inconvenience in working the sloop alone and have not lost a moment so far when sailing. My courage is better than it was and I am now at the edge of slipping off place.

I shall call at Fayal. The season is just right now to go without the wory from typhoons and monsoons. So I go east instead of west and roll around with the world. . . .

All the money I have been able to raise so far I have put into the Spray and into various absolute necessaries for the voyage

I think I shall begin now to knock things togather in better shape and follow a desided course—

I shall wait here for American mail. Sailing the first fair wind after that

Among the necessaries rounded up at Yarmouth was a tin clock priced at $1.50 "but on account of the face being smashed," Slocum bought it for $1. To clean and rate his chronometer, an instrument for measuring time where great accuracy is required, would have cost $15 which he did not have. So instead of a chronometer, a tin clock was his timepiece throughout the voyage. He also took a barrel of potatoes, butter, and six barrels of water on board.

On 2 July Slocum sailed from Yarmouth. He let go, as he wrote, his "last hold on America." The "boisterous Atlantic" was before him.

"About midnight the fog shut down denser than ever before. One could almost 'stand on it.' It continued so for a number of days, the wind increasing to a gale. The waves rose high, but I had a good ship. Still, in the dismal fog I felt myself drifting into loneliness, an insect on a straw in the midst of the elements. . . .

"During these days a feeling of awe crept over me. My memory worked with startling power. . . . I heard all the voices of the past laughing, crying, telling what I had heard them tell in many corners of the earth.

"The loneliness of my state wore off when the gale was high and I found much work to do. When fine weather returned, then came the sense of solitude, which I could not shake off. I used my voice often. . . . At the meridian altitude of the sun I called aloud, 'Eight bells,' after the custom on a ship at sea. Again from my cabin I cried to an imaginary man at the helm, 'How does she head, there?' and again 'Is she on her course?' But getting no reply, I was reminded the more palpably of my condition. My voice sounded hollow on the empty air, and I dropped the practise."

Instead of calling out orders, the captain took to singing; pitching his voice "for the waves and the sea and all that was in it." His "musical talent had never bred envy in others," he wrote, but he liked to sing. He sang the work songs of the merchant service, "Reuben Ranzo," "Johnny Boker," and "We'll Pay Darby Doyle for His Boots." He also sang hymns. In this way Slocum sailed eighteen days. When heard from next he had reached the Azores, the Western Islands, mariners called them. Three months had passed since he took his departure from Boston. Except for the worry of getting his copy in, things were going much better.

> "Spray," Horta Fayal
> 23rd July '95
>
> Dear Mr. Hardy: I have been trying to scribble a few lines for the newspapers, but find it almost impossible to do or to think The Spray is constantly crowded with these good Islanders.
>
> But I do hope the editor will make out something of what I send along. I will send in some other letter more detale of the voyage.
>
> The only surprise to me has been the contented state of my mind and my perfectly good health. Hope my friends are as well—
>
> I sail for Gibraltar tomorrow. This is the way to go round the globe: roll round with it!
>
> Very Sincerely
> /s/ Joshua Slocum
>
> U.S. Consul Genl sent a cable to the N.Y. World of my arrival here.

Slocum received a lively welcome from officials and everyday citizens. "It was the season for fruit . . . and there was soon more of all kinds of it put on board than I knew what to do with," he wrote. "Islanders are always the kindest people in the world, and I met none anywhere kinder than the good hearts of this place. . . . A damsel, as innocent as an angel, came alongside one day, and said she would embark on the *Spray* if I would land her at Lisbon. She could cook flying-fish, she thought. . . ."

Under way again and still his own cook, Slocum made an easy meal of fresh Pico cheese and fresh plums. Night found him lying on the cabin floor, sick with fever and cramps and delirious. Slocum had been reading Washington Irving's *Life of Columbus*. As the wind and sea rose and the *Spray* raced on, he saw the ghost of the pilot of the *Pinta* standing at the wheel of the sloop. For two nights and days the sloop sailed thus. "Columbus himself could not have held her more exactly on her course," Slocum wrote later. It was an early and unscheduled test of the *Spray's* extraordinary self-steering ability. When Slocum recovered, he found his ship heading as he had left her and then, "by inspiration" as he said, he threw overboard all the remaining plums.

I would guess that Slocum empathized with Columbus. Both the captain and the admiral had been past 50 when they embarked on their great adventures. Despite the many differences between the men and their times, Slocum was also on a voyage of discovery. He had a sense of his own adventure. "Early the next morning, August 4, I discovered Spain," he wrote. By evening he was inside Gibraltar.

At the British Colony, British naval officers gave the captain of the *Spray* a hero's welcome, and the *Spray* herself a berth among battleships. British sailors repaired the *Spray's* rigging. Fresh milk and vegetables sent by the admiral replenished her larder. Slocum went picnicking with the governor, sightseeing with the general. Nova Scotia born, the British loved him. Everywhere at Gibraltar he felt "the friendly grasp of a manly hand. . . ." He had landed at Gibraltar with $1.50 in his pocket but even that weak place received reenforcement. The treasurer and captain of the port loaned him $50 which Hettie, acting on Slocum's instructions, repaid a year later.

Part of Slocum's financial trouble arose through his inability to please the editor of the *Boston Globe*, the strong link in a weak syndicate. On 21 August the *Globe* reported, "Slocum Safe. . . .

The run to Gibraltar was . . . distinguished by a spell of bad
weather . . . ," but the *Globe* appears to have published only
three of his travel letters. His slow cautious pace and lack of
dramatic adventure did not make newspaper copy. He seemed
old-fashioned.

To the first piece, the *Globe* gave the heading, "Spook on
Spray. Ghost of Columbus' Man Steered the Boat. So Capt
Slocum Thought After Eating Plums and Cheese. But the Sloop
Reached Gibraltar Safely. Just 32 Days It Took the Yankee
Skipper. With Frolic Welcome the Brave Tar Greeted the
Tempests."

Slocum stayed at Gibraltar three weeks, and from there sent
the second of his published travel letters. It was not very good.
In an otherwise unoriginal report on the Rock, he told how near
the end of his visit he was guest of a party of naval officers on
board a torpedo boat. The talk turned to Slocum's countryman
and contemporary, Alfred Thayer Mahan, whose *The Influence
of Sea Power upon History 1660–1783*, was having a tremendous
effect on the naval mind.

"Capt Mahan's great book was praised. . . . One of the officers,
a wag, I suspected, incidentally remarked that the representative
present, from over the sea, looked like Capt Mahan. Acknowledg-
ing the compliment I simply said that 'I could stand it if Mahan
could.'

"What else could I say?

"The truth is, I think that I favor more our fellow-citizen Bill
Nye; with a secret fear that neither Mr. Nye nor myself would
be taken for handsome—in broad day."

Edgar Watson Nye (1850–1896), known as Bill Nye, was
another contemporary writer who may have influenced Slocum.
Born in Maine and reared in frontier country, his loud and obvious
humor was popular at the time. In 1895 he was writing for the
papers, the very thing Slocum aspired to.

As Slocum prepared to leave Gibraltar, British naval officers,
to his surprise, urged him not to proceed through the Mediterranean, the Suez Canal, and the Red Sea. The reason: pirates.
And under the very nose of Her Majesty's Navy! The route he
proposed would be extremely dangerous for a man alone. An

alternate eastward route was to sail around Africa. Slocum decided against it, doubtless to avoid the very long passage between the Cape of Good Hope and Australia. Running the easting down, as sailing men called it, was considered extremely hard and taxing. So Slocum had crossed the Atlantic for nothing. He would have to recross, and head westward after all.

13

*when I slept I dreamed
that I was alone*

In his third travel letter to the newspapers, Slocum recounted
what happened after he sailed from Gilbraltar on 26 August.
Moorish pirates lying off the coast of Morocco, spotted him as
he headed southwestward, more or less following Magellan's
course. Carrying all the sail he could, Slocum tried to outrun
them, while they, also crowding on sail, gave chase. Day was
ending and higher seas rolling up, conditions which favored the
Spray, Slocum thought—until a squall snapped her main boom.

"Here was I crippled in an instant and a craft coming down
on me. I didn't like it a bit," read the travel letter.

"I sprang instantly to the work of getting the broken boom on
board and of securing the sail. This I managed, I hardly know
how, but I recall that it was done quickly. And the sail was not
torn—a wonder!

"My presence of mind was good, and the machinery of the
head, such as it is, was working fast. I would have a hail now
in a moment more with the offer of help, maybe, as a beginning.

"It was the work of an instant to snatch rifle and revolvers up
from the cabin and be in readiness to discourage the plan. I was
bound to do without assistance so long as I had a shot left and
strength to fire it!

"When the boom broke my heart quailed, but now I was serene.
Having time to look around now, I saw the most gratifying change
in the aspect of affairs.

"The felucca—devil take him!—was dismasted outright. I felt
almost a disappointment.

"It took me, probably, a matter of two hours, in the rough sea, to mend the boom.

"The contrivance was simple enough, two bunk boards, two oars and a capstan bar lashed firmly over the broken part. . . .

"The quickest work at sea is always the best work."

After rewriting this episode in *Sailing Alone Around the World,* Slocum added, "By the time I had things in this order it was dark, and a flyingfish had already fallen on deck. I took him below for my supper, but found myself too tired to cook, or even to eat a thing already prepared. I do not remember to have been more tired before or since in all my life than I was at the finish of that day. . . . I fully realized now, if I had not before, that the voyage ahead would call for exertions ardent and lasting."

Ten days or so after leaving Gibraltar the *Spray,* as Slocum put it, "had settled down to the trade-winds and to the business of her voyage." Slocum signaled passing steamships and cattle-boats but received no answer. "The time was," he wrote, "when ships passing one another at sea backed their topsails and had a 'gam,' and on parting fired guns. . . . People have hardly time nowadays to speak even on the broad ocean. . . . There are no poetry-enshrined freighters on the sea now; it is a prosy life when we have no time to bid one another good morning."

An aging master in his chosen art, Slocum made the performance look easy. "My ship running now in the full swing of the trades, left me days to myself for rest and recuperation. I employed the time in reading and writing, or in whatever I found to do about the rigging and sails to keep them all in order. The cooking was always done quickly, and was a small matter, as the bill of fare consisted mostly of flyingfish, hot biscuits and butter, potatoes, coffee and cream—dishes readily prepared.

"When I slept I dreamed that I was alone . . . but, sleeping or waking, I seemed always to know the position of the sloop, and I saw my vessel moving across the chart, which became a picture before me."

After the trade winds, the doldrums. For 10 days and nights the *Spray* sailed, on average, only a mile and a quarter an hour. "The doldrums, I suppose you know," the captain explained to *Globe* readers, "are the baffling winds, light air, and heavy rain

squalls from all directions in the belt between the NE and the
SE trades . . . .

"I was greatly disappointed in the thunder and lightning in
the dolds this time crossing. I saw only one pale flash and heard
but the one most distant rumble. I must confess that I love to
hear it crash and shake the air all around. I do, indeed. I can give
no reason for the strange fascination, except that when a boy my
life was a burden of fear from the same mighty forces.

"Being taught to believe that lightning was to kill bad people
generally, and bad boys in particular, I naturally did some
trembling in those grand thunder storms that passed over the
old farm."

Forty days after leaving Gibraltar, Slocum reached the familiar
coast of Brazil. On 5 October he dropped anchor in the harbor
at Pernambuco, and three days later wrote Eugene Hardy, "I
lived awful hard coming down. But don't say anything about it."
Later, when he came to write *Sailing Alone Around the World*,
he glossed over his hardships and said, "Did I tire of the voyage
in all that time? Not a bit of it! I was never in better trim in all
my life. . . ."

In Pernambuco, recovering from the hard transatlantic voyage,
Slocum learned that his business of writing travel letters was
going badly. The *Boston Sun* was not taking any and the *Boston
Globe* was not buying at the anticipated price. Disregarding
punctuation more than usual, Slocum wrote Eugene Hardy.

Dear Mr. Hardy:—I recd. your kind note I am not surprised that a
letter of mine turned out bad, but Mr T—— [Charles Henry Taylor
(1846–1921)] agread on $20 per col for the availables not as a litterary
production—the high price—but to encourage the enterprise as I understood it and the editor of the Sunday Sun said "all right I'll go you $20"
that was all the contract mad[e]. the latter gentleman promise to give
me a note to that afect but seems to have forgotten it Mr Taylor, however, is doing what I expected to pay for: in manifolding editing etc—
no small job $5 per col or even less according to number of papers
would be all right. Mr T—— made the figures, not I.

The original list I have still. But please say nothing about it. I am
sorry. Would like at least to help my little boy.

The Sun printed trash of mine freely enough on more than one ocasion when it came for nothing. And I suspect that a case of murder or rape would find space for all the particulars, in all the papers.

But I can't go to war with them! . . .

I send one more letter I dare not look it over If it is not interesting, I can not be interesting stirred up from the bottom of my soul

It was the voyage I thought and not me. No sailor has ever done what [I] have done. I thank you sincerely for giving my son the money.

> Very truly
>
> Josh Slocum

I will report to you before sailing from here

Before setting sail again, Slocum made the first of a number of changes in the *Spray's* rigging. He shortened the main boom inboard four feet by removing the piece broken off when he ran from the pirates, and refitting the jaws. The change made the mainsail a little less cumbersome to handle.

Leaving Pernambuco on 24 October, Slocum continued south. Twelve hundred miles of sailing brought him to Rio de Janeiro where he picked up his mail. The word he received from the *Boston Globe* put an end to the travel letters. Perhaps Slocum was relieved. It is not surprising the venture failed but rather amazing it survived as long as it did. Very few of those who try it, succeed in keeping a diary while traveling. How much more difficult to write newspaper pieces while sailing singlehanded!

From the point of view of the *Boston Globe,* Slocum had been out seven months and what had he done? He had only begun his round-the-world circuit. His Atlantic crossings had canceled each other out. Slocum, who would require three years and more for his voyage, by now must have looked like a loser. Journalists like Nellie Bly who sped around the world in 72 days to beat the record of Phileas Fogg, hero of *Around the World in Eighty Days,* were what the crowd wanted in the 1890s.

On 11 November 1895, in Rio, Slocum wrote Hardy for the last time on newspaper business.

Dear Mr. Hardy: The Spray arrived here 5th, 12 days from Pernambuco. A good run considering the stormy head winds which she encountered to a very unusual degree

The Spray will refit and proceed South in a few days. The weather will be growing better ahead for the next two months.

If I find anything of interest to speak of before I tumble into the
Antarctic will write; but not to weary the papers nor to wory my best
friends

I shall always like to write to Messrs Roberts or to yourself if you
care to hear from me as I get along

I hav'nt, since the last news from Boston, felt like trying to write for
a paper I thought there was something in young C—— Taylor but I
find he is only a rich mans son after all.

I will not give your house any more surprises of the money order
kind. It was kind to advance the $20. I appreciate that and the books,
which I sold as I went along, and by them kept afloat. I am doing
better now and will be doing still better as I go along Treasure Island
is ahead!

I may arrive at Australia some day! You will surely want to hear
from the Spray at the great Southern Continent where our own language is spoken.

Will you please write me C/o U.S. Consulate Montevideo, Uruguay,
if there is anything to report? I have been more than paid for *three
Liberdade books* which I would like very much to have sent to the
enclosed addresses—if you will on the chances of getting your pay from
me later on

I will sell the balance of the edition by and by on satisfactory terms
I think. . . .

I am in the very best of health and living in great hope

I remaine Yours truly

                                                        Joshua Slocum

If Slocum wrote further to Eugene Hardy, or to Roberts
Brothers during the next two years, the letters have not come to
light; nor any word he might have sent Hettie, or his children.
By 1895, Victor was 23; B. Aymar, 22; Jessie, 20; Garfield, 14.

During his stay in Rio Slocum prepared to rig the *Spray* as a
yawl, the most convenient rig for single-handed sailing. He
mounted a bumkin, a semi-circular brace, over her stern to
support a jigger mast. He did not, however, step the mast. Placing
the mast and sail came later.

Slocum also made a stab at an old piece of business. He called
on government officials to ask for the wages due him for bringing
the *Destroyer* from New York to Brazil two years earlier. Political
fortunes, however, had changed since then. In 1893, the "legal

government" had hired Slocum but by 1895, Custodio de Mello's men, the former rebels, were in power. The latter, Slocum said, felt under less obligation to him than he could have wished. All they offered him was the gunboat herself where she lay, her smokestack awash in Bahia harbor. '

14

*I suddenly remembered
that I could not swim*

On 28 November 1895, Slocum sailed from Rio and headed south.
A few days later, coasting off Uruguay, the *Spray* ran aground on
hard sand. Using his makeshift dory and a small anchor, Slocum
tried to free the sloop. When that failed, he decided to try his
larger anchor. "The anchor, with forty fathoms bent and already
buoyed, I now took and succeeded in getting through the surf;
but my dory was leaking fast, and by the time I had rowed far
enough to drop the anchor she was full to the gunwale and sink-
ing. There was not a moment to spare. . . . I sprang from the oars
to my feet, and lifting the anchor above my head, threw it clear
just as she was turning over. I grasped her gunwale and held on
as she turned bottom up, for I suddenly remembered that I could
not swim.

"Three times I had been under water, in trying to right the
dory," Slocum wrote, "and I was just saying, 'Now I lay me,' when
I was seized by a determination to try yet once more, so that no
one of the prophets of evil I had left behind me could say, 'I told
you so.' Whatever the danger may have been, much or little, I
can truly say that the moment was the most serene of my life."

After almost drowning, Slocum managed to get himself ashore.
With the help of a nearby German rancher, "one soldier and one
Italian," he floated the *Spray*. Then, without further ado, the
sloop got under way again though somewhat the worse for the
pounding taken while lying on the sand.

Sailing into Montevideo, Slocum received a steam-whistle

welcome. "The voyage so far alone may have seemed to the Uruguayans a feat worthy of some recognition," he wrote, "but there was so much of it yet ahead, and of such an arduous nature, that any demonstration at this point seemed, somehow, like boasting prematurely."

At Montevideo the Royal Mail Steamship Company honored the Nova Scotia-born mariner with free dockage, free repairs, a gift of 20 pounds sterling "and more besides." Slocum was a hero to Britishers everywhere. "The calkers at Montevideo paid very careful attention to the work of making the sloop tight. Carpenters mended the keel and also the life-boat (the dory), painting it till I hardly knew it from a butterfly."

Ten years earlier Slocum had sailed the *Aquidneck* into Montevideo with Hettie, Victor and Garfield on deck and below, a cargo of case oil. He had been fairly well off and unknown. Now he was poor and becoming famous.

"Christmas of 1895 found the *Spray* refitted even to a wonderful makeshift stove . . . the pipe reached straight up through the top of the forecastle," Slocum wrote. "Now, this was not a stove by mere courtesy. It was always hungry, even for green wood; and in cold, wet days off the coast of Tierra del Fuego it stood me in good stead. . . .

"The *Spray* was now ready for sea. Instead of proceeding at once on her voyage, however, she made an excursion up the river. . . . An old friend of mine, Captain Howard of Cape Cod. . . . took the trip in her to Buenos Aires. . . . I was glad to have a sailor of Howard's experience on board to witness her performance of sailing with no living being at the helm. Howard sat near the binnacle and watched the compass while the sloop held her course so steadily that one would have declared the card was nailed fast. . . . The point I make for the *Spray* here, above all other points, is that she sailed in shoal water and in a strong current, with other difficult and unusual conditions."

Why was Slocum making this side trip up the Plata River to Buenos Aires? Surely not to demonstrate the *Spray's* self-steering qualities to Captain Howard, nor for the sake of the New England fish chowder Howard prepared on the way. Slocum made the trip sound like a picnic, but was it? Or was it in fact a pilgrimage?

Captain Slocum and Captain Howard must have sailed past the outer roads where the *Aquidneck,* with Virginia lying sick on board, had anchored 11 years earlier. Could he still see in his mind's eye the flag letter "J" flying from her mast, the signal that he was needed?

"I had not been in Buenos Aires for a number of years," Slocum wrote in *Sailing Alone Around the World.* "The place where I had once landed from packets . . . was now built up with magnificent docks." He told of being driven around the city and of going "in search of some of the old landmarks." Never a word concerning the English cemetery. Never a word about Virginia.

At Buenos Aires, Slocum unshipped the sloop's mast and shortened it seven feet. He also shortened the bowsprit by "about five feet" and later wished he had taken more off it. By trimming her wings, he made the *Spray* easier to manage.

Leaving Buenos Aires, 26 January 1896, Slocum sailed down the Plata to get on with the voyage. "I will not say that I expected all fine sailing on the course for Cape Horn direct," he wrote later, "but while I worked at the sails and rigging I thought only of onward and forward. It was when I anchored in the lonely places that a feeling of awe crept over me. At the last anchorage on the monotonous and muddy river, weak as it may seem, I gave way to my feelings." If Slocum had come from Virginia's grave, it was for the last time. He never saw Buenos Aires again.

Slocum headed into unfamiliar waters. "My ship passed in safety Bahia Blanca, also the Gulf of St. Matias and the mighty Gulf of St. George. Hoping that she might go clear of the destructive tide-races . . . I gave all the capes a berth of about fifty miles, for these dangers extend many miles from the land. But where the sloop avoided one danger she encountered another. For, one day, well off the Patagonian coast, while the sloop was reaching under short sail, a tremendous wave, the culmination, it seemed, of many waves, rolled down upon her in a storm, roaring as it came. I had only a moment to get all sail down and myself up on the peak halliards, out of danger, when I saw the mighty crest towering masthead-high above me. The mountain of water submerged my vessel. She shook in every timber and reeled under the weight of the sea, but rose quickly out of it, and rode grandly over the rollers that followed. It may have béen a minute that from my hold in the rigging I could see no part of the *Spray's* hull. Perhaps it was even less time than that, but it seemed a long while, for under great excitement one lives fast. . . ."

Speed, agility, physical strength and presence of mind are not enough in sailing. One must also be able to anticipate danger.

15

*a world behind . . .
another world ahead*

Early in February, 1896, the *Spray* reached and rounded Cape
Virgins, the eastern entrance of the Strait of Magellan. Though it
was the most favorable time of year, she encountered fierce currents and sudden squalls. "I reefed the sloop's sails," Slocum wrote,
"and sitting in the cabin to rest my eyes, I was so strongly impressed with what in all nature I might expect that as I dozed
the very air I breathed seemed to warn me of danger. My senses
heard '*Spray* ahoy!' shouted in warning. I sprang to the deck
wondering who could be there that knew the *Spray* so well as to
call out her name passing in the dark; for it was now the blackest
of nights all around, except away in the southwest where rose the
old familiar white arch, the terror of Cape Horn, rapidly pushed
up by a southwest gale. I had only a moment to douse sail and
lash all solid when it struck. . . . For thirty hours it kept on blowing hard. . . ."

The "smart breeze" which followed carried Slocum to Sandy
Point, Punta Arenas, a Chilean coaling station well inside the
Strait.

Slocum thought the inhabitants of Sandy Point, of mixed na-
tionality but mostly Chilean, not too badly off. "But the natives,
Patagonian and Fuegian, on the other hand, were as squalid as
contact with unscrupulous traders could make them," he wrote.
"A large percentage of the business there was traffic in 'fire-
water' . . . Fine specimens of the Patagonian race, looking smart
in the morning when they came into town, had repented before
night of ever having seen a white man, so beastly drunk were

they, to say nothing about the peltry of which they had been robbed." Slocum himself had never departed from the sober habit of his boyhood and first voyage.

The port captain at Sandy Point advised Slocum to ship a few hands to fight off Indians farther west in the Strait, but since no one cared to join him, Slocum loaded his guns instead. At this point an older sea captain stepped forward. Captain Pedro Samblich, "a good Austrian of large experience," presented Slocum with a bag of carpet tacks. "You must use them with discretion," Samblich said to Slocum, "that is to say, don't step on them yourself." Slocum got the message and, as he wrote, "saw the way to maintain clear decks at night without the care of watching." Samblich also asked Slocum to help himself from his (Samblich's) bottle of gold-dust but Slocum declined. "Samblich's tacks, as it turned out, were of more value than gold."

On 19 February, Slocum cleared Sandy Point. A little farther on, at Nicholas Bay, he encountered the first of the terrible squalls called williwaws. "They were compressed gales of wind that Boreas handed down over the hills in chunks." The next day, his fifty-second birthday, he was alone "with hardly so much as a bird in sight, off Cape Froward, the southernmost point of the continent of America." The following midnight, exhausted from fighting wind and water, Slocum dropped anchor in the lee of an island and made himself coffee. "Finding that the anchor held, I drank my beverage, and named the place Coffee Island," he wrote. "It lies to the south of Charles Island, with only a narrow channel between." Whether or not Slocum found an uncharted island, he had the pleasure of naming one, and a plain yet poetic, New England-sounding unvarnished name he gave it.

Days of beating against squalls and currents followed. When fair weather came it brought savages paddling canoes in pursuit. Thinking it inadvisable to let on that he was sailing alone, Slocum stepped into the cabin, crawled through the hold, and then came out the forward hatch, having changed his clothes on the way. "That made two men," he wrote. Next, he took the piece of bowsprit he had sawed off at Buenos Aires, and which he still had on board—he was not the man to throw good stuff away—and dressed it as a seaman. He arranged it forward and attached a line by means of which he could make it move. "That made three of

us . . . but for all that the savages came on faster than before."
Two shots, however, fired across their bows, sent them hurrying
back to shore.

When foul weather kept the Indians from venturing out in
canoes, Slocum on the opposite side of the Strait "went ashore
with gun and ax . . . and there felled trees and split about a
cord of firewood . . ." which filled his dory several times. With
every armful of wood he carried, he also carried his gun. "I have
described my method of wooding up in detail, that the reader . . .
may see that in this, as in all other particulars of my voyage, I
took great care against all kinds of surprises. . . ." Slocum's
method of wooding up was the same the early explorers used but
none of them wooded alone.

Sailing westward, making slow headway against winds and
currents, Slocum dropped and raised anchor many times. Looking
around as he beat his way between shores he called bleak and
unfinished, he saw no animals other than the Indians' dogs, and
an occasional seal. He noted few fish, and caught none. He said
he "seldom or never put a hook over during the whole voyage."
But he did dine "sumptuously" on mussels. And though he ob-
served "a sort of swan, smaller than a Muscovy duck" which he
might have shot, he did not raise his gun. "In the loneliness of life
about the dreary country I found myself in no mood to make one
life less, except in self-defense," he wrote. Throughout the voyage
Slocum fired only at sharks and men.

After ten days of uphill sailing, Slocum gained Port Tamar.
Cape Pillar at the western terminus of the Strait was in sight.
"Here I felt the throb of the great ocean that lay before me," he
wrote. "I knew now that I had put a world behind me, and that I
was opening out another world ahead."

On 3 March Slocum set out for Cape Pillar with a favorable
wind but it did not hold out. He had scarcely entered the Pacific
Ocean when the wind hauled northwest and turned into a very
hard gale—the same wind which 400 years before had driven
Drake south to discover Cape Horn. Slocum could not hold his
westward course. The *Spray*, her sails blown to ribbons, ran before
the wind. Under bare poles she headed southeast as though she
would round the Horn and carry Slocum back into the Atlantic. The waves "rose and fell and bellowed their never-ending

story of the sea; but the Hand that held these held also the *Spray*."
If Slocum lived by miracles, he did not count on them. He tried to
hold the *Spray,* too. He paid out two long sea ropes to steady his
craft and break the combing seas astern. He lashed her helm
amidship. But even "while the storm raged at its worst," he found
his ship "wholesome and noble. My mind as to her seaworthiness
was put to ease for aye."

On the fourth day of the gale, Slocum believed he was nearing
the point of Cape Horn. Through a rift in the clouds he saw a
mountain which he took for the Cape. That decided him to back-
track and go to the Falkland Islands in the South Atlantic to
refit. He headed east. Actually, however, he was still a hundred
miles north of the Cape, and instead of rounding it, was fetching
in towards the Cockburn Channel, one of the many arms of the
Strait. "Night closed in before the sloop reached land, leaving
her feeling the way in the pitchy darkness," he wrote. "I saw
breakers ahead before long. At this I wore ship and stood offshore, but was immediately startled by the tremendous roaring
of breakers again ahead and on the lee bow. This puzzled me
for there should have been no broken water where I supposed
myself to be. . . . In this way, among dangers, I spent the rest
of the night. Hail and sleet in the fierce squalls cut my flesh till
the blood trickled over my face, but what of that? It was day-
light, and the sloop was in the midst of the Milky Way of the
sea . . . and it was the white breakers of a huge sea over sunken
rocks which had threatened to engulf her through the night. It
was Fury Island I had sighted and steered for. . . . God knows
how my vessel escaped."

Charles Darwin, on board the British man-of-war *Beagle,* had
studied the region 50 years before Slocum saw it. "Our course,"
Darwin wrote, "lay south down that gloomy passage which I have
already alluded to as belonging to another and a worse world. . . .
Sir J. Narborough called one part South Desolation, because it is
'so desolate a land to behold'; and well indeed might he say so.
Outside the main islands, there are numberless scattered rocks on
which the long swell of the ocean incessantly rages. We passed out
between the East and West Furies; and a little further northward
there are so many breakers that the sea is called the Milky Way.
One sight of such a coast is enough to make a landsman dream

for a week about shipwrecks, peril, and death. . . ." Slocum, who had read *The Voyage of the Beagle*, said that Darwin might have added, "or seaman" as well.

Good luck followed bad. The Cockburn Channel led Slocum back into the Strait of Magellan near Cape Froward, a point he had passed weeks before, about midway between the oceans. "Every heart-beat on the *Spray* now counted thanks," he wrote. Doubtless for the first time in four or five days Slocum, anchored in a quiet cove, was able to cook. After "a hot meal of venison stew" (made of salt beef or salt pork), he was ready to sleep. "As drowsiness came on I sprinkled the deck with tacks," he wrote, "and then I turned in, bearing in mind the advice of my old friend Samblich that I was not to step on them myself. I saw to it that not a few of them stood 'business end' up; for when the *Spray* passed Thieves' Bay two canoes had put out and followed in her wake, and there was no disguising the fact any longer that I was alone.

"Now, it is well known that one cannot step on a tack without saying something about it . . . a savage will howl and claw the air, and that was just what happened that night about twelve o'clock, while I was asleep in the cabin, where the savages thought they 'had me,' sloop and all, but changed their minds when they stepped on deck, for then they thought that I or somebody else had them. . . . They jumped pell-mell, some into their canoes and some into the sea, to cool off, I suppose. . . . I fired several guns when I came on deck, to let the rascals know that I was home, and then I turned in again, feeling sure I should not be disturbed any more by people who left in so great a hurry." Skirting further dangers from williwaws, parting rigging, breakers, and rocks, Slocum got back to Sandy Point. There he turned the sloop westward again and for a second time set forth on the second half of the Strait.

Slocum's second attempt to reach the Pacific did not go unrewarded. In a cove some miles west of Borgia Bay,* he dis-

---

* A latter-day sailor, Felix Riesenberg, wrote: "Passing Big Borgia, or Despair Island, we were looking on the unspoiled world of steep mountains, icy crags, and terrifying rocks that first met the eyes of Magellan. . . . I came upon a small indentation, the famous spot where ships for long had been in the habit of leaving visiting cards, boards on which were painted

covered "wreckage and goods washed up from the sea." He guessed that the gale which had driven him towards Cape Horn and into the Cockburn Channel had washed the wreckage ashore and driven the Indians away. He worked all one day salving and boating the goods to the sloop. Most of it consisted of "tallow in casks and in lumps from which the casks had broken away." There was also a barrel of wine. Slocum wrote, "I hoisted them all in with the throat-halyards, which I took to the windlass. The weight of some of the casks was a little over eight hundred pounds." At this place he had to fill "a barrel of water at night," and he took time to measure a giant stalk of kelp, "roots, leaves, and all, . . . one hundred thirty-one feet in length."

Slocum worked till the *Spray* was fully loaded. "I was happy then in the prospect of doing a good business farther along on the voyage, for the habits of an old trader would come to the surface. I sailed from the cove . . . greased from top to toe, while my vessel was tallowed from keelson to truck. My cabin, as well as the hold and deck, was stowed full of tallow, and all were thoroughly smeared."

Some years later, when Slocum was home, in telling a friend of the voyage, he said: "When I was rounding the southern point of Patagonia we [sic] had severe cold weather and I felt the need of fatter food than I'd been having. Luckily about that time I secured some barrels of very fine tallow . . . and I began to fry buns and doughnuts in that tallow. Here's one of my buns on the mantel now. It looks and feels just like a rock, doesn't it? I must put it in a safer place. Some burglar will be breaking in here after jewelry and take this. It's the last specimen I have and I wouldn't want to lose it."

Twenty-six miles west of the cove where the *Spray* took in tallow lay Port Angosto, "a dreary enough place" but a haven where Slocum could refit and clean up his boat. "I carried on sail to make the harbor before dark, and she fairly flew along, all covered with snow, which fell thick and fast, till she looked like a white winter bird," he wrote.

At Port Angosto Slocum fitted the jigger mast to the bumkin,

their names and the dates of their anchoring. Among the lot, many rotting away, was the name of Captain Slocum's brave little *Spray*." (*Cape Horn*, New York, 1939, pp. 364–5.)

the brace he had set on the stern of the *Spray* at Rio five or six months earlier. With a jigger mast and a third sail ready, the *Spray* was now rigged as a yawl. "I called the boat a sloop just the same," Slocum wrote, "the jigger being merely a temporary affair." Few things, however, prove more permanent than temporary arrangements. The sloop *Spray* remained a yawl to the end.

In addition to fitting the jigger at Port Angosto, Slocum also mended his sails and rigging, took in wood and water, put his cabin "in better order," and transferred the cargo of tallow from the deck to the hold. All the while he kept his rifle beside him and every night spread tacks on deck.

Slocum wrote he "remained at Port Angosto some days." It must have been about a month. After six attempts to reach the Pacific only to be driven back each time by adverse winds, he decided to wait for the change of season. "In the first week in April southeast winds . . . bringing better weather . . . began to disturb the upper clouds; a little more patience, and the time would come for sailing with a fair wind."

On 13 April, more than two months after first entering the Strait, Slocum weighed anchor from Port Angosto for the seventh time. As he stood at the wheel that day, the *Spray* (for he gave her the credit) "cleared the great tide-race off Cape Pillar and the Evangelistas, the outermost rocks of all. . . ." She did not do it unassisted. "I remained at the helm," Slocum wrote, "humoring my vessel in the cross seas. . . . I did not dare to let her take a straight course. It was necessary to change her course in the combing seas, to meet them with what skill I could when they rolled up ahead, and to keep off when they came up abeam."

The following morning found Slocum still at the wheel. To seals and sea birds he shouted, "Hurrah for the *Spray!*" As what must have been a long afternoon was ending, and evening came on, a wave, "larger than the others that had threatened all day,—one such as sailors call 'fine-weather seas,'—broke over the sloop fore and aft." It also broke over the man at the wheel. "It seemed to wash away old regrets. All my troubles were now astern . . . all the world was again before me," Slocum wrote. "The wind was even literally fair." By this time Slocum had stood at the wheel and guided his boat for 30 hours on end. Now with a fair wind and plenty of sea room the *Spray* could be left to sail herself while he went below.

The English geographer, W. S. Barclay, in his book, *The Land of Magellan,* noted that among all the voyages made through the Strait, three will not be forgotten. The first is that of the discoverer. The second, Sir Francis Drake's. Drake, without charts, made it through the Strait in 16 days. The third is Joshua Slocum's. Barclay calls Slocum's "in point of pure seamanship" the most remarkable of all. Slocum both sailed and navigated alone. At the western entrance, he single-handed survived a Cape Horn equinoctial gale. He passed an entire night cruising and tacking in what are acknowledged as among the most dangerous waters in the world. Finding his own way to re-enter the Strait, he sailed again to Cape Pillar, thus circumnavigating "the wildest part of desolate Tierra del Fuego" and as treacherous a triangle as any mariner could ask for.

The single-handers who came after Slocum took other routes and, since 1915, have gone through the Panama Canal. Slocum's now legendary passage through Magellan country has not been repeated nor his account of it equaled.*

* In his anthology of classic New England literature, *A New England Reader* (1962), Van Wyck Brooks included from *Sailing Alone Around the World,* Slocum's chapters on the Strait of Magellan, in company with extracts from Longfellow, Emerson, Hawthorne, Thoreau, Dana, Prescott, Higginson, Dickinson, Beston, etc., etc.

16

*then was the time
to uncover my head*

Almost a year to the day had passed since the *Spray* first set sail.
Back in Boston a few may have wondered what had become of
Slocum. He had no way of letting anyone know that, alive and
well, he was on the Pacific. "Then was the time to uncover my
head," he wrote, "for I sailed alone with God. The vast ocean was
again around me . . . the *Spray* was under full sail, and I saw
her for the first time with a jigger spread. This was indeed a
small incident, but it was the incident following a triumph. The
wind . . . had moderated, and roaring seas had turned to gossip-
ing waves that rippled and pattered against her sides as she rolled
among them, delighted with their story."

Slocum steered for Juan Fernandez—Robinson Crusoe's island,
he called it—and 15 days out, on 26 April, made it dead ahead.[*]
"The blue hills of Juan Fernandez," he wrote, "high among the
clouds, could be seen about thirty miles off. A thousand emotions
thrilled me when I saw the island, and I bowed my head to the
deck. We may mock the Oriental salaam, but for my part I could
find no other way of expressing myself."

Slocum's response to the islanders was to offer them Yankee
hospitality. He asked them to come on board the *Spray* where he
served them coffee and doughnuts, the latter fried in tallow.

[*] *The Life and Strange Surprising Adventures of Robinson Crusoe* by
Daniel Defoe was based on Alexander Selkirk's solitary sojourn on Juan Fernandez. Selkirk (1676–1721) was a Scotsman who ran away to sea. In
1704, after a quarrel with his captain, he was put ashore at his own request on the then uninhabited island. He was rescued in 1709.

"They were so benighted," he explained later, "they'd never seen a doughnut in their lives." By evening of his first day on the island, he had taught the islanders how to make and fry them. He then sold them tallow as fast, he said, as he could weigh it out. "I did not charge a high price . . ." he wrote, "but the ancient and curious coins I got in payment . . . I sold afterwards to antiquarians for more than face-value. In this way I made a reasonable profit. I brought away money of all denominations . . . and nearly all there was, so far as I could find out."

Slocum took his time at Juan Fernandez. Hurrying was not his way, and besides there was nothing to hurry for. "Blessed island of Juan Fernandez!" he wrote. After stretching his legs for ten days, on the day before his departure, the island children, "one and all," went with him gathering wild quinces, peaches, and figs. "I got some nice quinces on Robinson Crusoe's island, and when I left I put them into preserves as I sailed along," he recalled.

Slocum sailed on 5 May 1896. He headed north and after passing the island of St. Felix, picked up the trade winds. The winds blew hard and the *Spray*, under reefed sails, sped westward "with a bone in her mouth." When the forward motion of a vessel creates white foam at her bows, she is said to sail with a bone in her mouth.

"My time was all taken up those days—not by standing at the helm; no man, I think, could stand or sit and steer a vessel round the world: I did better than that; for I sat and read my books, mended my clothes, or cooked my meals and ate them in peace. I had already found that it was not good to be alone, and so I made companionship with what there was around me, sometimes with the universe and sometimes with my own insignificant self; but my books were always my friends. . . .

"I sailed with a free wind day after day, marking the position of my ship on the chart with considerable precision; but this was done by intuition, I think, more than by slavish calculations. For one whole month my vessel held her course true; I had not, the while, so much as a light in the binnacle. The Southern Cross I saw every night abeam. The sun every morning came up astern; every evening it went down ahead. . . . If I doubted my reckoning after a long time at sea I verified it by reading the clock aloft

made by the Great Architect. . . ." Seeing the Southern Cross
every night now must have brought memories of Virginia.

In spite of the losses incurred in the past, there still was much
to be thankful for. "I awoke, sometimes, to find the sun already
shining into my cabin. I heard water rushing by, with only a thin
plank between me and the depths, and I said, 'How is this?' But
it was all right; it was my ship on her course, sailing as no other
ship had ever sailed before in the world. The rushing water along
her side told me that she was sailing at full speed. I knew that
no human hand was at the helm; I knew that all was well with
the 'hands' forward, and that there was no mutiny on board."

On the 43rd day from Juan Fernandez, "a long time to be at
sea alone," the peaks of Nukahiva, one of the Marquesan islands,
thrust up from the horizon. Unbelievably, Slocum did not pause
but instead pressed on. He wanted to reach Samoa to pay his
respects to Mrs. Robert Louis Stevenson, the widow of one of his
favorite authors.

Little disturbed Slocum's daily routine as he sailed westward.
"I was *en rapport* now with my surroundings, and was carried on
a vast stream where I felt the buoyancy of His hand who made
all the worlds." He was startled by a near collision with a whale.
He fired at sharks that came too close. "Nothing is more dreadful
to the mind of a sailor . . . ," he wrote, "than a possible encounter with a hungry shark." The companionship of the birds
must have meant a great deal; he wrote they were always around.
Sometimes a bird would perch on the mast of the *Spray*. During
all the long time he was crossing the South Pacific from Juan
Fernandez to Samoa, Slocum did not sight a ship.

In *Sailing Alone Around the World*, Slocum wrote that on the
long passages at sea he ate "potatoes and salt cod and biscuits"
and always had plenty of coffee, tea, sugar, and flour—typical
Yankee rustic fare. He made his biscuits two or three times a
week. Several years later, however, when interviewed as to how
he managed his meals, he gave a more detailed account. "There
is great chance for missionary work in cooking," he told Clifton
Johnson (1865–1940), New England folklorist, illustrator and
photographer. Johnson published the interview in an article called
"The Cook Who Sailed Alone."

"When I started on the voyage . . . ," Slocum said, "I laid in two barrels of ship's bread, or pilot bread, as some call it. In appearance this bread is like a large thick cracker of rather coarse quality. There's no nonsense about it, though. It was made for keeps. It isn't fine and white like the crackers most people like to buy. You could eat a bushel basket full of those and get no substance. But this old-fashioned hard bread is a kind of whole wheat. . . . My two barrels full lasted me the voyage through. I put them up in tin cans while they were dry and crisp, and I sealed the cans with solder so the bread was as good three years old as it was new.

"I used to soak my hardtack and make bread pudding of the very nicest kind and it had strength and nourishment, too. It was something that would stand by you. I soaked the bread about six hours to get it thoroughly soft, then added sugar, butter, milk and raisins, put it on my lamp-stove and in a few minutes it was done.

"My stores included . . . baking powder, salt, pepper and mustard—yes, and curry, I mustn't forget that. Curry powder is great stuff aboard a vessel. It was just what I needed to give the final touch to my venison stews that I made out of the salt beef and salt pork I carried along. Besides those meats I had ham and dried codfish. The fish wasn't any of those little tom cods, skinned and bleached and tasteless, that most people fancy, but big fellows, thick as a board and broad as a side of sole leather. Very few persons know how to treat a salt codfish properly. To freshen it they let it stand in water half a day or more, very likely, and it may be, use several waters. That takes all the goodness out. You can get rid of the extra salt just as effectively and without hurting the fish by picking it to pieces and washing it with your hands— just shaking it up and down in the water. Then put it right into the pot and boil for fifteen minutes. When you get it ready for the table, add butter and pepper and chop a hard-boiled egg and put on top. You take codfish cooked that way and I want to set down prepared to hoist in a meal of it; and all I want besides is potatoes, coffee, and bread and butter."

In addition to his Boston salt cod, Slocum enjoyed fresh fish even though he seldom if ever angled or trolled. In the tropical waters through which he did most of his traveling, fish came aboard on their own. "Ah! such breakfasts as I used to have," he recalled when he no longer had them. "Often I'd get up in the

morning and find a dozen . . . flying fish on the deck, and sometimes they'd get down the forescuttle right alongside the frying
pan."

In his rambling fashion Johnson revealed Slocum's day-to-day
mealing while sailing alone. Slocum's domestic arrangements were
characteristically simple and sound. He knew the importance of
eating the right things. He explained how he made his soda bread,
and the biscuits he was so fond of. When it was time for a mug
up, he knew just how he wanted his coffee. "I ground my own
coffee . . . that's the only way to have it good. Ground coffee
isn't worth as much by a great deal if you've let it stand for a day.
Add your hot water and serve at once. You mustn't boil it."

The milk the captain used was condensed but unsweetened. He
called it "evaporated cream." When he laid in a supply of butter,
he would fill all his "tumblers and mugs with it, spread a thin
layer of salt on top and then tie a bit of muslin over that." The
butter would then be placed in what he called a strong pickle.
"Butter in brine like that," the captain said, "will keep as long as
you want." As for eggs, the captain said he had more of them
than one would imagine. He kept them by immersing them in hot
water for a minute. "That hermetically sealed the pores," he explained, "and they would be all right for a good many weeks,
even in a very hot climate."

Best of all were the potatoes, that "highly prized sailors'
luxury." One pictures Slocum eating them three times a day. "My
potatoes were usually delicious," he said. "I never got up those
frothy varieties they call 'creamed potatoes.' No, sir, I advocate
cooking the potatoes and bringing them to the table with their
jackets on, unless they throw them off themselves in the process
of cooking. That's the natural way, and that's the only way to get
their full virtues."

Slocum lived and sailed on this limited diet continuously for 73
days, his longest passage without touching land. Almost two and
a half months with only the unbroken ocean to look at, without
seeing a soul or hearing a human sound. He dropped anchor at
Apia in the kingdom of Samoa on 16 July, at noon. Yet even after
that long and maybe tedious time at sea, he did not step ashore
at once. Instead, he spread an awning on deck and sat in its shade
a while, listening to Samoan voices drifting across the harbor.

Three young women in a canoe paddled out. "Talofa lee (Love to you, chief)," they hailed him. Slocum called it a "naive salutation." Then they looked at the flag which flew from the *Spray*. "Schoon come Melike?" Yes, Slocum told them, he had come from America.

" 'What for you come long way?' they asked."

"To hear you ladies sing."

" 'Oh, talofa lee!' they all cried, and sang on. Their voices filled the air with music that rolled across to the grove of tall palms on the other side of the harbor and back."

Fanny Stevenson came down next day to greet the captain and invite him to Vailima, the Stevensons' struggling tropical plantation. When he arrived she asked if he wished to sit at the desk Stevenson had used but Slocum could not bring himself to do it. Slocum admired Fanny Stevenson. She had shared many voyages with her husband. He had once had such a wife.

Mrs. Stevenson presented him with four volumes of sailing directories for the Mediterranean which later he may have read but never found a chance to use. She inscribed them,

"To Captain Slocum. These volumes have been read and re-read many times by my husband, and I am very sure that he would be pleased that they should be passed on to the sort of seafaring man that he liked above all others.

Fanny V. de G. Stevenson"

As he sailed farther from "the center of civilization"—did he mean Boston?—Slocum "heard less and less of what would and what would not pay." He wrote, "Mrs. Stevenson, in speaking of my voyage, did not once ask me what I would make out of it." He delighted in a Samoan chief who said to him, "Dollar, dollar, white man know only dollar."

These reflections on the white man's values did not interfere in any way with business as usual. The voyage was paying off in various ways not foreseen. Before he left the islands Slocum sold the last of his tallow to a German soap-maker. He also delivered a message from the publisher, Adam Wagnalls, to the Samoan king. "The good King Malietoa," Slocum wrote, "notwithstanding that his people have not eaten a missionary in a hundred years

. . . seemed greatly pleased to hear so directly from the publishers of the 'Missionary Review.'" Toloa, the princess, "a sort of
Queen of the May," gave Slocum a bottle of cocoanut oil for his
hair, a gift the bald-headed Joshua wrote, "another man might
have regarded as coming late." Fanny Stevenson, for a farewell
present, gave him a couple of bamboo trees which he later used
for extra spars.

Samoans, Slocum wrote, "have great reason to love their country and to fear the white man's yoke." He called Samoan life a
poem. "While the days go thus in these Southern islands we at
the North are struggling for the bare necessities of life." Some
men might have lingered long at Samoa, some remained always.
Slocum, however, stayed only a month. He still had miles to go.

On 20 August 1896, Slocum weighed anchor and the *Spray*
stood out to sea. Feeling very lonely as the islands receded and
faded, Slocum resorted to his old remedy—making himself as busy
as possible. He crowded on sail and steered for "lovely Australia"
with its memories of 25 years before. Virginia's kin waited to welcome him. But again not a word of Virginia got into his book. In
Sailing Alone Around the World he wrote only that Australia was
"not a strange land" to him. Another 42 days of sailing, much of it
through storms and gales, carried him over the International Date
Line, clear across the South Pacific to Newcastle, New South
Wales.

17

*in the teeth of
a gale of wind*

Slocum arrived at Newcastle "in the teeth of a gale of wind" early in October. Almost a year and a half had elapsed since he last saw Boston; he was half way around the world. He had already accomplished what no sailor known to history had done before.

News of the record-breaking voyage had been gathering momentum and, traveling faster than the *Spray*, preceded her to Australia.

Australian newspapers of those days, reflecting a pioneer outlook of settlers in a new-old land, usually took a critical and even hostile view of a stranger reaching their shores. An exception, however, was made of Slocum. Australians responded warmly.

When "The Pilot" of the *Sydney Daily Shipping News* heard that Slocum, coming from Samoa, had made the Australian seaboard at Newcastle, in a boat no bigger than a typical Sydney harbor sloop, he burst into song.

> Hear the song of skipper Slocum
> Best afloat.
> This is not a Yankee Fairy
> Anecdote,
> But the plain unvarnished story
> Of a seaman bold and hoary
> Who set out in search of Glory
> In a boat.
> All alone he sailed from Boston
> One fine day
> In a swagger little lugger
> Called the *Spray*,

> Bound to cross the broad Atlantic
> (True a most peculiar antic!)
> Even tho' the gales were frantic
>   Every day.
> All's well however that ends well
>   They say:
> Which applies to skipper Slocum
>   And the *Spray*.
> Therefore let us sing their praises
> (Like we do all other crazes)
> In a manner which amazes
>   Hip, Hooray.

A native of Nova Scotia, Slocum was a born British brother to Australians. He had the British heart of oak, something the *Sydney Morning Herald* appreciated.

"No doubt the daring exploits of Captain Joshua Slocum are unique and he is not likely to have many imitators; but of admirers and sympathizers there are legion. And this could hardly be the case if the ideal were not still at the long last and in the deep inner heart of humanity a more powerful motive than the real—if adventure and danger, now as formerly were not regarded as finer qualities than comfort and ease. If that were not really so, those gallant voyagers who make such persistent efforts to reach the North Pole would be regarded as hopeless lunatics, Stanley would probably have been set down as a monomaniac with a partiality for African wanderings, and as for Captain Slocum—well, Captain Slocum would have to be placed in a special class of derangement by himself. But, as we know, this is not the attitude of the world at all. . . . Captain Slocum is feted by British squadrons and hailed everywhere as a worthy descendant of an illustrious line of sea-kings. And so probably it will be to the end of time; the highest intellectual development is not likely ever to lessen the delight which we all naturally feel in stirring action—in worthy deeds worthily carried to an end.

". . . in the voyage of the *Spray* we see acute and thoughtful intelligence permeating the requisite courage of the navigator. . . . It proves that two conspicuously British qualities, method and adventure, are still active; and that a man if he have a strong purpose and a strong heart may live to himself for twelve months or so in a cockleshell on the storm-tossed seas, even in these days of overpowering luxury."

Concerning his stay at Newcastle, Slocum wrote only, "Many visitors came on board, the first being the United States consul, Mr. Brown. Nothing was too good for the *Spray* here. All government dues were remitted, and after I had rested a few days a port pilot with a tug carried her to sea again. . . ."

Slocum did not say that while he was resting, a ghost of his old career came to life. Henry A. Slater, ex-convict and former second officer on the *Northern Light,* was living in Sydney. Hearing that his one-time commander had docked at Newcastle and soon would be coming to Sydney, Slater prepared to get even with him. He was still very bitter about the 53 days spent in the brig under Slocum's orders. Slater denounced Slocum at public meetings. He also gave out his story "in his own words," and in harrowing detail to the *Sydney Daily Telegraph.* The paper published it on the eve of Slocum's arrival in Sydney.

"In the year 1883 I signed articles as second mate of the ship *Northern Light,* then under the command of Captain Joshua Slocum, at Port Elizabeth, South Africa. In the course of conversation the captain told me that he had a very mutinous crew, and that as the other officers were afraid of the men he wanted an officer of my stamp to keep them in order. He gave me to understand that I was to be a regular 'Bucco,' or bully, on board," said Slater.

"Shortly after I had come on board, the next morning, I heard Mrs. Slocum, the captain's wife, scream, and running to the gangway found that one of her children had fallen overboard. I jumped over after the child, as also did a man in my watch named Hansen, and succeeded in saving the child and bringing it safely on board. The harbor, I may state, is infested by sharks. Mrs. Slocum was effusive in her thanks, but the captain never mentioned a word about the matter.

"All went smoothly until the day before we started on the voyage to New York, whither we were bound. The captain and first mate being ashore I was in charge of the ship. I told the third mate, M'Quaker, to do a job with some of the crew forward. Shortly afterwards I heard a row, and going forward, saw M'Quaker unmercifully beating one of the crew. I remonstrated with him, whereupon he answered me in a very insulting manner, and said that my time would come when we got to sea. I ordered him to his cabin, when he began to use most disgusting language, and on his way aft kicked a boy whom he passed, saying at the time that he was one of my favorites. I was so incensed that I gave him a thorough thrashing. The captain and mate came on board a little later, and M'Quaker was for some time closeted with Slocum.

"Some days after we had sailed from Port Elizabeth, Captain Slocum came to me and asked me when I 'was going to start on the crew,' explaining that I had said that I would play the deuce with the men when we got to sea. I intimated that I was not prepared to beat and ill-treat the men for his satisfaction, as I found them good seamen and respectful and obedient. I also warned him that if he ill-treated any of the men I would be a witness against him. He went away muttering to himself. About a fortnight after leaving port the captain came up while I was directing a job on the mizzen mast, and found fault with the work. I pointed out that I was competent to do the work, and had satisfactorily superintended the same work on the fore mast. He had a sheath knife in his hand, and he rushed over and struck at me. I caught his hand, twisted the knife out of his grasp, and threw it overboard. He then went below.

"That evening I slipped and fell, fracturing my right ribs, and the next day called the captain and told him that I would have to lay up. He replied that he would have no loafing on his ship, that he would disrate me, and ordered me forward to the forecastle. I told him that he dared not disrate me, when he rushed at me, knocked me down, and kicked me about the face and head. I was carried forward by the other officers, and placed in a berth in the forecastle. The next morning the captain, first and third mates, carpenter, and boatswain dragged me on deck, and the captain spat at me and struck me in the face with a belaying pin. I managed to crawl back to the forecastle, and then fainted. When I woke up in the evening the men held a consultation, and agreed that they would not stand by and see me ill-treated in the manner I had been.

"The men began arming themselves and sharpening their knives, but I begged of them not to interfere, as the officers were armed, and I feared that there would be bloodshed. I entreated them not to interfere with the captain and officers, pointing out that they would be severely punished as mutineers if they did, and I would be charged as the ringleader. At first they would not listen, but eventually I got them to promise not to interfere, whatever happened, but to take note of everything, taking day and date, so that when we reached port we could have justice meted out to us.

"The next morning the captain and officers and carpenter and boatswain came forward, armed with revolvers and cutlasses, and handcuffed my hands behind my back. They then threw me down the half-deck, and kept me there all day without food or water. About midnight I wrested my hands free, and crawled on deck, and into the mate's cabin, where I secured a revolver. After deliberating for some time, I threw the revolver overboard and went forward and lay down.

"About 8 o'clock the following morning the carpenter came to the forecastle and nailed up one of the doors and the shutter. Then the captain and his officers and petty officers came forward and ordered all the men on deck. The officers then began to fire their revolvers into the forecastle. Fortunately I was not struck by any of the bullets. After a time the mate, Mitchell, called upon me to surrender. He was afraid to enter the forecastle for some time, but at last came in when I told him that I was unarmed. He told me that the trouble would blow over, and that he would see me reinstated as second mate. I got up, and he helped me to the door. When I got out on deck I was seized from behind, knocked down, and two pairs of handcuffs were put on my wrists. I was then dragged aft to the poop, where shackles were put on my ankles. A chain was then placed round my throat, crossed behind my neck, wound around my body under my arms, down through the handcuffs, down through my legs, then up to the back of my neck, and made fast. Then a length of chain was made fast to the shackles on my ankles, and the whole lot of chain rivetted together. I had then over 80 lb. of chain on my body.

"The captain then told the carpenter to partition off a portion of the lazaret for my reception. This was beneath the cabin, and there was a passage in the 'tween decks on each side of the cabin about 4 ft. wide and 4 ft. deep. One end was nailed up, and I was dragged up and thrown down the hatch into the lazaret. The captain then ordered the other end to be boarded up. I was then in a space 4 ft. by 4 ft., and 5 ft. long. I am 5 ft. 10 in. in height, so I had not too much room in which to lie down. I could not reach my mouth with my hands on account of the chains. A hole was cut in one of the boards, and one end of the chain attached to my ankle was pulled through and made fast to a stanchion outside my 'box.'

"At first my daily fare was one ship's biscuit and a half pint of water. That did not kill me, so the same amount of biscuit and about three or four tablespoonsful of water was tried. Still I did not die. For the first three weeks in this 'box' I suffered the tortures of the damned, my hunger and thirst were intolerable. I begged Captain Slocum to give me water and food; but in vain.

"After I had been for about thirty days in the box I heard Mrs. Slocum playing a hymn on the organ. She played, 'Nearer, My God, to Thee,' and I joined in, and began to sing. Suddenly, while I was singing, the chain attached to my ankles was hauled up to the hole, bringing my feet up about three feet from the deck. I was kept in this position for over three days without food or water. At the end of that time the captain came down fully armed to see me. He let my legs down again.

"I begged of him to give me some water. He laughed, and said, 'Are you very thirsty, old man? Very well, I will give you a good drink if you promise to behave yourself.' I promised I would not sing again, and he went and got me a big dipper of water. I said, 'God bless you, Captain Slocum, for your kindness in bringing me this water.' I then began to drink, and found that he had given me a dipper of sea water. I had drunk quite a quantity before I ascertained that the water was salt, and naturally my thirst was increased a hundredfold. The next day I received my usual allowance of water and biscuit.

"I began to find the rats troublesome about now. I would often wake up and find them running all over me, and even biting my skin—I had no flesh. I wondered why they came after me, as I was nothing but skin and bone. I soon found out. I frequently fancied about this time that I could smell butter or melted cheese. I found out later on that Captain Slocum used to pour melted butter or cheese on to what remained of my clothes to attract the rats.

"After I had been about 40 days in the box, a large rat was running over me, and I succeeded in catching him in my hands. I was in such a desperate state of hunger that I squeezed the life out of the rat, and then ate it. I never, however, managed to get this change of diet again.

"My box was never once cleaned out for the period of 53 days during which I was confined therein, nor was I allowed to wash myself. After the first couple of weeks I broke out into a rash, and found that I was covered with vermin. The rats had almost stripped me of my clothing, and were often gnawing at my legs and arms. Captain Slocum would occasionally come down, bringing with him bread and meat or cakes or doughnuts, show them to me, and then deliberately eat them before me. Shortly before we arrived in New York, the captain brought down some carbolic acid to disinfect my box, and sprinkled some on my body and face, drops falling in my mouth and eyes.

"On arriving at New York I was arrested and tried for mutiny, and honorably acquitted. Captain Slocum and his two mates were then arrested, and were each severely punished for their cruelty to me. The captain was fined 500 dollars and the mates 100 dollars each.

"I ask the public before making a god of this man to wait until I am placed face to face with him. I do not make these statements to gain notoriety, or even sympathy, but simply to show my fellow-citizens what kind of a man they are dealing with in Captain Joshua Slocum."

To be sure there was a tough side to Slocum but was he capable of this cruelty? To what extent was Slater's story true?

After publishing Slater's side of it, the paper sent a reporter to interview Slocum. The reporter wrote that Slocum does not deny that he imprisoned Slater, but this was done, he says, "only after the latter had broken out of the stateroom, where he was first confined for insubordination. Captain Slocum alleges that, though ironed and placed in a stateroom, Slater broke out of his place of confinement and armed himself. He also states that he (Slater) attempted to incite the crew to mutiny. Thereupon he (Captain Slocum) had him ironed and imprisoned in an apartment specially built for the purpose in the lazarette. Captain Slocum declined to make any set statement in reply to the allegations of Slater, but he placed at the disposal of your reporter a book containing a number of clippings from American papers referring to the case of the *Northern Light*. These included an account of an interview between the reporter of a paper called the 'Telegram' and a sailor who served on board the *Northern Light* at the time Captain Slocum commanded her, and Slater held the position of third mate. This man, in his statement, contradicted Slater in his story of his imprisonment and treatment by Captain Slocum on board the *Northern Light*. The man in question, a sailor named Dimmock, expressed to the reporter his opinion that Slater was, although a bad man, not cruelly treated by Captain Slocum. The interview with Dimmock resulted in a number of charges being laid against Slater on the score of competency and conduct generally as a ship's officer. Clippings from other American papers go to support the captain's contention that Slater, and not he, was in fault in the trouble that took place on board the *Northern Light*. Captain Slocum says that he does not fear a complete investigation of the whole affair. He readily admits that the American courts fined him $500 for his action in regard to Slater, the whole of which his underwriters paid; but he urges that the judge summed up in his favor when placing the case before the jury, and expressed the belief that he (Captain Slocum) did not act with malice or with motives of revenge, but was actuated merely by a desire to maintain discipline and to bring his ship safely into port. Copious extracts from newspapers published in America at that time to a large extent support Captain Slocum's statements."

How much there was to all this is impossible to say but it should not be suppressed or dismissed. Grossly exaggerated stories may have a basis in fact. A master in sail with his family aboard could have overreacted to trouble.

Seemingly unperturbed, Slocum got ready to leave Newcastle. He had accommodated himself to the demands of Nature, to winds, seasons, and seas; but he would not alter his plans to avoid a threatened showdown. The very next day after learning of Slater's charges, Slocum sailed for Sydney.

18

*time flew fast those days
in Australia*

Slocum sailed into Sydney harbor on the evening of 9 October, into the waiting arms of the harbor police. "I came to in a snug cove . . . ," he wrote in *Sailing Alone*, "the Sydney Harbor police-boat giving me a pluck into anchorage while they gathered data from an old scrap-book of mine. . . . Nothing escapes the vigilance of the New South Wales police. . . . Some said they came to arrest me, and—well, let it go at that."

In spite of not feeling well—the result of having been inadvertently struck on the head by a heavy rope en route—Slocum took hold of the problem with Slater right away. Slocum had him summoned to Water Police Court where he and Slater confronted each other. Slocum told the magistrate, Mr. G. W. F. Addison, that he did so to preserve his life and person, that he had known the defendant some time, and that he believed him to be a man who might carry out a threat. Slocum said he had heard that Slater had told a crowd, "This Captain Joshua Slocum, God help him when we meet. I'll not be responsible for my actions. This man you are making an angel of, I'll make an angel of him when I get hold of him."

The hearing continued with Slater then cross-examining Slocum:

"Slater: Who gave you the information?
"Mr. Addison: Don't answer that question.
"Slater: Will you swear that this action has not been taken out of malice?

"Mr. Addison: What is the use of asking such a question? The complainant has already said that he wants protection from certain threats you are alleged to have made.

"Slater: I don't know the law.

"Mr. Addison: Well you ought to. Were you not a policeman?

"Slater: You have been here for ten days, and have I done you any harm?

"Mr. Addison: What's the use of asking such a question?

"Slater: Is this not the first time you have seen me for about thirteen years?

"Captain Slocum: I have not seen you for about that time.

"Slater: Are you afraid of me?

"Captain Slocum: Well, you are a most excitable man, and, from the language you have used, you might possibly do me an injury. I certainly am, to a certain extent, afraid of you.

"Slater: You ought to be at least morally afraid of me.

"George Walker,* clerk, said he heard the words set forth in the information used by the defendant at the Queen's Statue on the afternoon of the 7th instant.

"Slater: I did not speak at the Statue on that day.

"Detective Rochaix said that he had heard the defendant use the following when addressing a crowd, at the General Post Office: 'Captain Slocum is a coward. He daren't meet me face to face. But I will force him to meet me.'

"Slater then made a statement denying that he had used the words of which he was accused."

When the hearing ended, the magistrate's decision was that Slater keep the peace six months, and also put up 80 pounds as security that he would do so.

The matter did not end there; in spite of the decision in Water Police Court, Slater went on addressing public meetings. "Feeling is running very high . . . and the city promises to be divided into sections over this alleged ill-treatment of 13 years ago," the *Daily Telegraph* said. Slater was speaking "in language which not only showed an almost frenzied earnestness, but which also sug-

* George Washington Walker, Virginia's brother, was Slocum's brother-in-law.

gested a lively contempt for the libel law. Slater expressed the desire to meet Captain Slocum on the public platform. . . . He promised that he would shortly procure chains and shackles, and exhibit himself as he says he was bound on the *Northern Light.*"

Slocum was interviewed again by the *Daily Telegraph.* Asked about Slater's charges, "the captain said he was very much disgusted that any credence should be placed in the statement made. He hinted that there was some sinister and hidden purpose in the statements, but no amount of pressing would induce him to be more explicit. He, however, showed our representative further writings from newspapers, exonerating him from all blame in the affair. . . .

" 'My whole life,' he said, 'is open to inquiry; and I do not think anyone can prove a dishonorable action against me. I, however,' he continued, 'hardly like accepting the hospitality of the Sydney people, after this attempt of Slater's to blacken my character. If I was guilty of what he accuses me, I would be ashamed to land in your city. I will later expose the falsity of the accusations, and lay bare the motives of the accuser.'

"Captain Slocum was looking fairly well, though a bit haggard."

A few days later, headlines read, "Reception of Captain Slocum / The Spray Towed Up the Harbour / Congratulatory Address." Feelings ran high and people took sides.

A reception committee chartered the steamer, *Minerva,* and with about 130 people aboard, set out from Circular Quay, crossed Sydney Harbor, and steamed to the cove called North Harbor where the *Spray* lay at anchor. Slocum was on deck, aft, and in response to the cheering on board, dipped his flag. Some of the Walker family, who had come out with the party, went aboard the *Spray.* When they returned "the formal part of the proceedings took place. . . ."

Slocum was brought on board the *Minerva,* and enthusiastically cheered. A Mr. F. B. Evans spoke. He said that he wished "on behalf of those who had assembled there to extend to Captain Slocum a hearty and cordial welcome. He thought that they were entitled to greet Capt. Slocum in this manner as a yachtsman and as an intrepid navigator, who had achieved the feat of travelling round the world alone (applause). They had heard different things about Captain Slocum, but they were only there to welcome him as a daring man who had travelled over all seas without even anyone to stand to the main sheet (applause). . . ."

A telescope and a badge were presented to the captain. He replied with "a few words to express his thanks for the reception that had been accorded him. . . ."

Not everyone admired Slocum. There were dissenters in the ranks.

"The Johnstone's Bay Sailing Club had specially chartered the Balmain steamer *Lady Manning* to follow some races which took place on that day. At the termination of the races, she steamed down to Bradley's to enable her passengers to have a look at the *Spray*. As she lay a short distance away, some of the reception committee appealed to some of the crowds which covered her in every part, to give Capt. Slocum a cheer. But there was a profound silence on the steamer. Eventually one of the committee standing on the bridge of the *Minerva*, shouted . . . 'Now then, Balmain people, three cheers for Captain Slocum.' This forcible appeal was answered by some hostile display, although some of the *Lady Manning* passengers waved their hats. Another appeal only produced additional boo-hooing and although the receptionists on the *Minerva* lustily cheered at the same time, they were not of sufficient strength to outweigh the hostile demonstration. . . ."

Like any other topic of the hour the controversy ran its course and the altercation blew over. Within a month Slocum had settled into his usual sociable life when in port, receiving callers, accepting invitations, and also sometimes sending regrets. The following letter was sent me from Australia by P. R. E. Murnin.

Manley Nov 11th 96 *

The Spray
Frank J. Donovan Esq:—

Dear Sir

I was not able to avail myself of the honor to attend the Balmain Annual Regatta Prince of Wales Birthday

The friend whom I had engaged to care for the Spray could not come and circumstances wer such that I could not bring the beloved old craft along.

* Manly is a suburb to the north of Sydney.

I regret very much at having missied so much

Thanking you Sir for your courtesy I am truly yours

/s/   Josh Slocum

Like many who travel alone, Slocum reached out and made friends on the way. "Though I do not feel oppressively lonely on my solitary voyage, I am always glad to get to port. I am, paradoxical as it may seem, really a sociable man . . . ," he told a reporter.

Slocum's unusual voyage appealed to a broad range of people; many wanted to help. He needed new sails, and no sooner did he make his wants known, than a new suit of sails appeared at the cabin door, the gift of Mark Foy, Australian department store founder and yacht club commodore. Slocum bent on the new canvas but did not jettison the old. He was too canny and thrifty for that. He may already have had in mind the ingenious use to which he would later put it.

19

I trusted now to the mercies
of the Maker of all reefs,
keeping a good lookout
at the same time
for perils on every hand

It was early summer in Australia when the *Spray*, sporting her new sails, left Sydney on 6 December bound for Melbourne. "The *Spray* paid no port charges . . . anywhere . . . ," Slocum wrote, "till she poked her nose into the customhouse at Melbourne, where she was charged tonnage dues. . . . The collector extracted six shillings and sixpence. . . ." Slocum more than made up for it by charging people for coming on board. He then caught a shark and asked extra for looking at that. The income from this exhibition—Slocum called it "a good show"—added to what he had made on the tallow, sent him to the bank to deposit money. He did not say how much, but it must have been a great improvement over the $1.50 he had started out with.

Adverse winds and ice drifting up from the Antarctic forced Slocum to change his plans from sailing below Australia to sailing above it. Whichever way he went he would be on his way home. While waiting for the season of favorable winds needed to take him through Torres Strait, across the top of Australia, he decided to make a side trip to Tasmania. None of his earlier voyages had taken him there though he had sailed around it. Burford Sampson of Pennant Hills, New South Wales, and who formerly lived in Tasmania, wrote me his recollections of Slocum's visit.

". . . The unexpected arrival of the *Spray* at the mouth of the

Tamar River caused much excitement in the town of Launceston, when the news was received from Low Head Pilot Station that Captain Slocum intended to sail her up to the town, some 44 miles away. The Tamar is one of the few rivers in the world which is navigable for vessels of 5,000 tons from its mouth to its source—tidal, with a rise of from eleven to fourteen feet, on the ebb with a current of some six or seven knots. It is a splendid waterway, two to three miles wide in places—at its source is Launceston, a town at the time of the Yankee skipper's visit of some 20,000 souls. He sailed her up without a pilot. During his stay of a week or so—the little craft was thrown open for inspection and he gave two or three lectures in a public hall on his single handed voyage, which filled us schoolboys with wonder and not a little awe. . . . The citizens headed by the Mayor, gave Slocum a civic welcome and the lecture hall was packed to the doors at all his lectures.

"The Captain was exceedingly good to us kids, marking our atlases for us with his log and telling us of his experiences when passing through the Straits of Magellan. . . . He told us he was never lonely and that well out on the ocean, he always turned in at night without any fears and had a good night's sleep, knowing the little *Spray* would not let him down. He said he found peace in the midst of the ocean. . . . He said '*Spray* is a fine sea boat'; this we found hard to imagine for her draught was very shallow. . . . We also thought she would not be much good to windward, but he said she was not bad and a good all rounder. To us, this dry humourous Yankee was a hero, and we worshipped accordingly. Also, before he went away. . . . we prevailed on our mothers, cousins, and aunts to come to light with jams, jellies and other not perishable grub, to stock up the *Spray's* larder. . . ."

In Australia, Slocum learned to show off the *Spray;* in Tasmania, how to lecture. He delivered his first talk in a hall in a town near the mouth of the Tamar. The owner, "a kind lady from Scotland," gave him free rent.

A Tasmanian gentleman gave him free advice. In his first attempts on the platform, Slocum said he felt uneasy. His newfound friend reassured him. "Man, man," he said to the captain, "great nervousness is only a sign of brain, and the more brain a man has the longer it takes him to get over the affliction. But you will get over it." In recalling the helpful words several years later,

Slocum added that he thought it "only fair to say" that he was not yet quite cured.

By displaying his boat and speaking about his travels Slocum found a new way to make a living. "As in many other of my enterprises," he wrote, "I had gone about it at once and without a second thought."

Tasmanians took to Slocum. One day, while he was away from the *Spray,* he returned to find a letter on board. He opened it and read "A lady sends Mr. Slocum the enclosed five-pound note as a token of her appreciation of his bravery in crossing the wide seas on so small a boat, and all alone, without human sympathy to help. . . ." The lady did not call again nor did he learn who she was.

For his part, Slocum "was haunted by the beauty of the land-scape all about. . . . If there was a moment in my voyage when I could have given it up, it was there and then. . . ."

Four months later, on 16 April 1897, Slocum was once more under way, northward bound, his patience rewarded by fine weather. He settled down to reading day and night, and left that "pleasant occupation" only to trim sail, or tack, "or to lie down and rest, while the *Spray* nibbled at the miles." He compared his state with that of circumnavigators of olden times. "Their hard-ships and romantic escapes—those of them who escaped death and worse sufferings—did not enter my experience, sailing all alone around the world. For me is left only to tell of pleasant experi-ences, till finally my adventures are prosy and tame."

Not quite. A few days later, Slocum rounded Great Sandy Cape on Australia's east coast and reached the gateway of the Bar-rier Reef. "At last here was the *Spray* in the midst of a sea of coral. . . . I trusted now to the mercies of the Maker of all reefs, keeping a good lookout at the same time for perils on every hand."

Running before the trade winds, Slocum sailed "the Barrier Reef and the waters of many colors studded all about with en-chanted islands!" Peacefully he passed among those islands. He stopped to give a lecture at Queensland. At Cooktown, where he moored the *Spray* nearly abreast of the Captain Cook monument, and saw "the very stones the great navigator had seen," he lec-tured for charity in the Presbyterian Church. He made Thursday Island, mid-channel in Torres Strait, on 22 June, and as the only

American Victorian in port, helped celebrate the Diamond Jubilee of the Queen's reign—a jubilee with an Australian corroboree in it. Ten days later, he sighted the large island of Timor to the north; on 11 July, Christmas Island was abeam. Slocum had reached the Indian Ocean.

It was now only 550 miles to the Keeling or Cocos Islands but unless he navigated with great accuracy, he would miss the tiny atoll. Slocum made the islands dead ahead. "The first unmistakable signs of the land was a visit one morning from a white tern that fluttered very knowingly about the vessel, and then took itself off westward with a business-like air in its wing. . . . Farther on I came among a great number of birds. . . . My reckoning was up, and springing aloft, I saw from halfway up the mast cocoa-nut trees standing out of the water ahead. I expected to see this; still, it thrilled me as an electric shock might have done. I slid down the mast, trembling under the strangest sensations; and not able to resist the impulse, I sat on deck and gave way to my emotions. To folks in a parlor on shore this may seem weak indeed, but I am telling the story of a voyage alone."

Slocum dropped anchor in the island lagoon 17 July. He stayed several weeks. From there he wrote Joseph B. Gilder, the editor who had praised *Voyage of the Liberdade*, heading the letter: "The *Spray* tied to a palm-tree at Keeling-Cocos Islands Aug 20th 1897." *

Perhaps you did not expect to get a letter from this little kingdom in the sea; but one never knows what may happen and the risks one runs—on the land.

Keeling Cocos is a strange little world owned by the first settlers, a family of Scotch of the name of Cluenis-Ross Many things here are the reverse of other lands and the women, to use a homely phrase, rule the roost. It comes hard on the men. It would do the soul of the wretched Fuegan woman good to see the Keeling "lord and master" up a cocoanut tree. I am looking over these things as I sail along. The heart of a missionary is all on fire to reconstruct the religion of this people. If ever one sets foot on this peaceful land, I hope he will not be of the soul-destroying sort that spoiled my earley days—

* The letter was addressed, Joseph B. Gilder, N.Y. Critic, 287 Fourth Ave., New York. I bought it in 1952.

The conversation with yourself, once, often comes to mind, about our thoughts at sea. While I may not think cleare I am certainly clearer at sea than in a busy city and the thing most on my mind, that is, the business in hand, the reckoning, as I sailed along has been better kept than ever before on any ship of mine soever well officered. Was it from being even more alone in my case.

Looking over the journals of all the old voyagers I see non, working the old fashioned methods, so nearly correct as the *Spray* has been in making her land-falls—seven times now in succession. I never did better when I had even the best of chronometers and officers to assist—now will you tell me where it comes in? my "chro" is a one-dollar tin clock! And of course is almost no time piece at all—I have to boil here often to keep her at it, from noon to noon,* through the months.

Some thinking man will help me out on this else I will never be able to explain how it is done—The one thing most certain about my sea reckonings: They are not kept with slavish application at all and I have been right every time and seemed *to know* that I was right; Even a lunar observation (so fare have taken only one on the voyage) taken, of course, alone, was practically correct, I found, a few hours later, when I made the land.

There was not a difference of five miles between Lunar obvs dead reckoning and the true position of the vessel asuming the longitude of the Marqueses to be correct. I was then 43 days out and had not lost 6 hours rest But the vessel had sailed at her top speed all that time or all the time that the wind blew hard.

Your N.Y. ladies I see are going in for yachting

Why not study navigation too? A lady, in your city born, used to stand on deck and take good "sights" and work them, too, as correctly as any one could do †

My plan, to be useful, will be to sail a "college" ship around the world!

How I would like to teach young people in the science of Nautical Astronomy

A fine sailing ship would be my choice & she should be a flyer making steamboat time without the bustle of steam and all its discomforts

I smile at some of the comments made on my present insignificent "outing" Some think I am exploring the resourses of a man under great disadvantages. They are most all very kind in their comments but most all wrong as to the real object of my voyage which to tell the truth I

* On shipboard the day begins at noon.
† Another reference to Virginia. Though raised in Australia, she had been born in New York.

did not think would interest our people; so I merely remarked before shoving off that I was going alone

What I sailed for I have got, and more I found things I did not dream of meeting with I hoist them all in—have worked harder in port than at sea—I have now a valuable cargo—Sail tomorrow homeward.

Do you think our people will care for a story of the voyage around?

Postmarked Batavia, 29 September 1897, the letter was not received until 3 November. Slocum had been away 28 months and not much had been heard from him. Gilder had asked Slocum's lawyers, Cowen, Wing, Putnam & Burlingham, a well-known New York firm specializing in admiralty cases, what they knew of his whereabouts. They replied that the most recent word had come from Melbourne, 17 January. "He does not say when he is coming home. He says that he is writing now and then to the N.Y. *Sunday World*," they added.*

During the months he was away, to whom did Slocum write? Hettie? If so, the letters have not survived. A sister of Hettie's, Mrs. J. W. Tingley of Brighton, Massachusetts, wrote me that Hettie "destroyed many of the Captain's letters, etc., before she left here the last time . . . her mind was failing during the last years."

Did Slocum communicate with his children? No letters are mentioned in Victor's biography of his father. Though Victor saved letters, I saw none from his father among his papers. B. Aymar wrote me, "I believe J. S. wrote mostly to me—and often." But no letter to B. Aymar from the years of the round-the-world trip survives. In answer to my question, Jessie wrote, ". . . about any letters I might have received from father . . . if I did they were destroyed many years ago." Garfield wrote me he never in his life had a letter from the captain.

On 24 August 1897, two days after Slocum left Keeling Cocos, homeward bound, the *New Bedford Evening Times* reported, "Probably Lost. Family of Capt. Josiah [sic] Slocum Relinquish All Hope . . . Believed That He Was Drowned During a Heavy Storm."

"Providence, Aug. 24—Capt. Josiah Slocum, who sailed from

* I have not been able to find anything Slocum wrote for the *New York Sunday World*.

Boston April 24, 1895, with the intent of circumnavigating the globe in a cockle shell, is probably lost. His daughter, who lives in Attleboro, has heard nothing from him in some time, and it is believed that his little boat *Spray* has been overcome in an ocean storm. Captain Slocum kept those at home posted as to his movements and when the weeks and then months passed without word of any kind from him the fear became the belief that he was no more. . . ."

But not long after that, the *New York Evening Post* had a different report on the voyage of the *Spray:* ". . . The Little Sloop with Capt. Slocum at Port Louis, Mauritius."

"Port Louis, Island of Mauritius, September 21.—The forty-foot sloop *Spray,* Capt. Joshua Slocum, of Boston, Mass., has arrived here on her way around the world. . . ."

"The sloop was now drawing near the limits of the trade-wind," Slocum wrote later, "and the strong breeze that had carried her with free sheets the many thousands of miles from Sandy Cape, Australia, fell lighter each day until October 30, when it was altogether calm, and a motionless sea held her in a hushed world. I furled the sails at evening, sat down on deck, and enjoyed the vast stillness of the night."

After the calm came gales as severe as any Slocum had weathered except off Cape Horn. It was 17 November before he could make the harbor for Durban, Port Natal, South Africa. On a letterhead of the Royal Hotel, Durban, Natal, 9 December 1897, he wrote Roberts Brothers.

Dear Sirs:—I mailed papers to yourselves from ports on the way also from this place, reporting the Spray

By this mail I send you P.O. Order for £5—about the amt, with interest, I hope, that you paid my son Victor, some time ago ($20)

My ambition is to pay all my little debts before I reach home. I see no reason, now, why I shall not be able to do so

I had quite a long pull to get at what I am about now—I shall have reason to remember some of my old friends *

I met Stanley, here, the other day.† I was at the time, a guest of

---

* Slocum drew his pen through this sentence.

† Sir Henry Morton Stanley (1841–1904), English-born explorer, came to the United States in 1859 and adopted the name of his employer. His writings include *How I Found Livingstone,* 1872; *Through the Dark Con-*

Colonel Saunderson, M. P. Stanley is M. P. you remember It is said that he can do more by keeping quiet than any man alive

He wanted to know what I would do without compartments if the Spray should strike a rock? "Must keep her off the rocks." "If a swordfish should run her through? what then?" "That *would* boom my show" Stanley must have been bored for he gave a smile that would make a worried editor yell with envy—

We all had coffee then and Irish Stories. Stanley however gave a recipe which I think he said was American; perhaps it is old—I don't know: to keep intoxicating fumes down if one must drink: "take, first, a wine glass of oil" that, of course, rises over the liquor—One of the party was an old sea captain and told the worst story, so the Colonel declared that was ever heard and appealing to me asked if ever I heard "so bad a yarn?" It was a bad story, even for a sea captain and I admitted that I never heard a worse except some that I myself had told

Stanley smiled again that angelic smile born of practice and of long years of observation—

The best told story of the evening was accorded me! You may see that we had a wretched time! However the Col said it was all right, and thereupon invited me to put up at Saunderson Castle and make that my home when I come to Ireland, which certainly I shall do

With kind regards

Yours as always

Joshua Slocum

Unaware that the papers back home had him lost at sea, Slocum was having a splendid time hobnobbing with the elite.

tinent, 1878; and *In Darkest Africa,* 1890. He made his last trip to Africa in 1897.

20

the sloop was again
doing her work . . .
leaping along
among the white horses

Christmas 1897. Slocum wrote that the *Spray* "was trying to stand on her head. . . . She began . . . to pitch and toss about in a most unusual manner, and I have to record that, while I was at the end of the bowsprit reefing the jib, she ducked me under water three times for a Christmas box. I got wet and did not like it a bit: never in any other sea was I put under more than once in the same short space of time. . . . A large English steamer passing ran up the signal, 'Wishing you a Merry Christmas.' I think the captain was a humorist; his own ship was throwing her propeller out of water."

A few days later, the gale having moderated, Slocum was able to clear the Cape of Good Hope peninsula. "The voyage then seemed as good as finished; from this time on I knew that all, or nearly all, would be plain sailing."

Slocum dropped anchor in the bay off Capetown. Given a free railroad pass by the government, he explored the South African colonies, visited Kimberley and Johannesburg, and toured the gold fields of the Witwatersrand. At Pretoria he shook hands with President Kruger.* One of the party mentioned that their guest was on his way around the world. Kruger, who believed the world was flat, corrected him. "You don't mean round the world,

* Stephanus Johannes Paulus Kruger (1825–1904), president of the South African Republic for four terms, 1883–1900. He was known as "Oom Paul."

you mean in the world," the old statesman said, and "glowered" at Slocum. Everyone felt embarrassed, except Kruger and Slocum. The latter was delighted with "the nugget of information quarried out of Oom Paul. . . ."

"It sounds odd to hear scholars and statesmen say the world is flat, but it is a fact that three Boers of considerable learned ability prepared a work to support that contention," Slocum wrote in *Sailing Alone*. "While I was at Durban they came from Pretoria to obtain data from me, and they seemed annoyed when I told them that they could not prove it by my experience. . . . The next morning I met one of the party. . . . I bowed and made curves with my hands. He responded with a level, swimming movement of his hands."

After hundreds of miles of travel over the plains of South Africa, Slocum returned to the dock in Capetown where he had left the *Spray*. He found her waiting, just as he had left her and with everything in order. "I have often been asked," he wrote, "how it was that my vessel and all appurtenances were not stolen in the various ports where I left her for days together without a watchman in charge. This is just how it was: The *Spray* seldom fell among thieves. At the Keeling Islands, at Rodriguez, and at many such places, a wisp of cocoanut fiber in the door-latch, to indicate that the owner was away, secured the goods against even a longing glance. But when I came to a great island nearer home, stout locks were needed; the first night in port things which I had always left uncovered disappeared, as if the deck on which they were stowed had been swept by a sea."

On 26 March 1898, Slocum sailed from South Africa. A steam tug towed the *Spray* out to sea which gave her a good offing, but then the wind died away and Slocum and the *Spray* were left "riding over a heavy swell, in full view of Table Mountain and the high peaks of the Cape of Good Hope. On the second day a favoring breeze came up. "The wind was from the southeast; this suited the *Spray* well," Slocum wrote, "and she ran along steadily at her best speed, while I dipped into the new books given me at the cape, reading day and night. March 30 was for me a fast-day in honor of them. I read on, oblivious of hunger or wind or sea, thinking that all was going well, when suddenly a comber rolled over the stern and slopped saucily into the cabin, wetting

the very book I was reading. Evidently it was time to put in a
reef. . . .

"March 31 the fresh southeast wind had come to stay. The
Spray was running under a single-reefed mainsail, a whole jib,
and a flying-jib besides, set on the Vailima bamboo. . . . The
sloop was again doing her work smoothly, hardly rolling at all,
but just leaping along among the white horses. . . ."

Very early in the morning of 11 April, as the *Spray* sailed up
the South Atlantic Ocean, a quacking booby awakened Slocum.
"It was as much as to say, 'Skipper, there's land in sight' . . . and
sure enough, away ahead in the dim twilight, about twenty miles
off, was St. Helena." Slocum reached for his bottle of wine in the
locker and drank the health of his "invisible helmsman—the pilot
of the Pinta."

Slocum stayed ten days at St. Helena. He followed a pattern
by now become almost routine; sight-seeing, lecturing, dinners
with the governor, and then the farewell gifts of fruits and cakes.
But at this departure he received, as well, a rather singular
offering: a goat. The animal would be companionable as a dog,
he was told.

Except for the first day out, before "the beast got his sea-
legs on," Slocum was not happy with his companion. The goat
"threatened to devour everything from flying-jib to stern-davits."
He was the "worst pirate" encountered on the voyage. One day,
while the captain was on deck, the critter, in the cabin, ate the
West Indies charts. "Alas!" Slocum wrote, "there was not a rope
in the sloop proof against the goat's awful teeth!" He and the
goat parted company at Ascension Island, the next port of call
and discharge. The goat was the last of a small band of fellow-
travelers; a spider, a tree-crab, a rat, a centipede, a pair of
crickets—none of which survived long.

Three days at Ascension were enough. Slocum had reached
the backstretch; the voyage was speeding up. Passing at night
south of Fernando de Noronha, a Brazilian island group 200 miles
offshore, the *Spray* "crossed the track, homeward bound, that she
had made . . . on the voyage out. . . ." Though still in the South
Atlantic and 4,000 miles from home, Slocum had come full circle.

Once more the old familiar waters. Breezing along the coast of
Brazil, the *Spray* sailed where the *Aquidneck* and the *Liberdade*

had left their tracks. "Strange and long-forgotten current ripples pattered against the sloop's sides in grateful music. . . . I sat quietly listening . . . ," he wrote.

Slocum sped north. He was making almost 200 miles a day and had crossed the equator when on 14 May he suddenly saw a mast "with the Stars and Stripes floating from it, rising astern as if poked up out of the sea, and then rapidly appearing on the horizon, like a citadel, the *Oregon!*"

The Spanish-American War had begun. Though Slocum had heard in Capetown there might be a war, he had no way of knowing it had actually come. The battleship *Oregon*, in command of Captain Charles E. Clark, was hurrying to join the Atlantic fleet. When Slocum saw her—a thousand times the size of the *Spray*—charging up astern of his little vessel, he could not at first make out what her signals were saying because *he had no binoculars*. When the *Oregon* passed ahead, however, he read her flags, C B T, meaning, "Are there any men-of-war about?" "No," Slocum signaled in reply and added, he had not been looking for any. The final signal, Captain Slocum to Captain Clark, "Let us keep together for mutual protection." But this, in Slocum's words, the commander of the *Oregon* "did not seem to regard as necessary. . . ."

Sadly missing the charts the St. Helena goat had eaten, Slocum steered for the Caribbean. When he found himself among mysterious breakers, he had to rely on memory, knowledge of the sea, and the craft which had brought him thus far. At one point breakers almost boarded the sloop. "But you'll go by, *Spray*, old girl!" Slocum said he shouted in the night. She did go by and then, he wrote, he "slapped her on the transom, proud of her last noble effort. . . ."

Arriving at Grenada he was waylaid promptly by a reporter, but apparently the conversation was brief. Slocum on his way to a meal cooked ashore, "was not altogether in the mood to be pestered by an interviewer," wrote the newspaperman. In Grenada, Slocum lectured to a full hall; and a week or so later, repeated the performance further north, at Antigua.

Slocum left the West Indies on 5 June, bound for a United States port, the last leg of the voyage. "The *Spray* was booming along joyously for home now," making good time, when suddenly

she struck the horse latitudes. There was not a breath of wind.
For eight long days the captain was becalmed. The sea was so
smooth that evening after evening he could read on deck by the
light of a candle. Under such circumstances, a less self-sufficient
man might have been swallowed up in the solitude of waiting.
But Slocum knew "a philosophical turn of thought now was not
amiss, else one's patience would have given out almost at the
harbor entrance."

The final calm of the voyage preceded one of the final storms.
On 20 June, a gale was blowing, "accompanied by cross-seas that
tumbled about and shook things up with great confusion." The
Spray's rigging gave way. The jib-stay broke at the masthead, and
jib and all fell into the water, but Slocum managed somehow to
rescue his gear. Then, with cool nerve and unbelievable agility
the 54-year-old sailor climbed the swaying mast and made the
repairs. There was no one at the wheel to steady the vessel.

But he was "tired, tired, tired of baffling squalls and fretful
cobble-seas." He had not seen a ship for days. "As to the whistling
of the wind through the rigging," he wrote, "and the slopping of
the sea against the sloop's sides, that was well enough in its way,
and we could not have got on without it, the *Spray* and I; but
there was so much of it now. . . ."

On 25 June, Slocum was heading toward Fire Island when a
tornado struck. He had seen it coming and was ready for it. The
climax storm of the voyage he called it. Up to that point he had
been bound for New York, but when the storm was over, he
changed course.

H. S. Smith of Port Washington, New York, then a cabin boy
on board a sloop about two miles to windward, and caught in
the same blow, saw the yawl-rigged *Spray*. "We saw her start
sheets and head in an easterly direction . . . ," Mr. Smith wrote
me many years later. "Of course we did not recognize the *Spray*
at that time, but later we realized that the little yawl we saw
must have been the *Spray* from the fact that she carried not the
customary gaff-headed sail but a balanced or 'standing' lug on
the jigger. This sail was so rare in the United States—in fact, is
so now—that the vessels carrying it can be numbered on the
fingers of one hand."

Slocum steered for Newport, Rhode Island. The weather was

fine and only one danger remained. Newport harbor was mined.

"The *Spray* . . . ," Slocum wrote, "was safe enough so long as she hugged the rocks close, and not the mines. Flitting by a low point abreast of the guard-ship . . . some one on board of her sang out, 'There goes a craft!' I threw up a light at once and heard the hail, '*Spray*, ahoy!' . . . I eased off the main-sheet now, and the *Spray* swung off for the beacon-lights of the inner harbor." At one o'clock on the morning of 27 June 1898, Slocum ended his voyage. He had sailed some 46,000 miles; spent three years, two months, and two days.

21

*I had . . . a desire
to return to the place
of the very beginning*

Stepping ashore in the land of his citizenship, Slocum had to make himself known. The Spanish-American War had all but totally eclipsed his achievement. The papers were much too busy to play up an aging offbeat sailing master. Slocum could not make the front page even in Newport. Page 3 of the *Newport Herald,* 28 June 1898, said, "Early yesterday morning a staunch-looking little craft swung lazily into the harbor and cast anchor off Commercial wharf. She was a stranger in these waters and her rig . . . attracted the attention of the early risers. . . . The solitary occupant of the boat busied himself in making everything neat and tidy aboard ship and appeared to be totally oblivious of the curiosity he was arousing. When the master of the craft had prepared everything to his satisfaction he jumped into a dory and sculled ashore." The *Boston Globe* covered Slocum on its last page. New York papers gave him scant notice; the *Times* none at all. Slocum had not changed the course of history though he had, in his way, made a little.

The reception was different from those he was used to. Nothing but the uncomprehending stares of idlers on the waterfront greeted him and the *Spray.* Americans were wary of what seemed a tall tale. Some called the circumnavigation a fake—until Slocum produced the *Spray's* yacht license stamped in every port she visited. Former associates in the merchant service hinted that coming from South Africa, Slocum might be a diamond smuggler.

Others, however, believed his story. Within 24 hours a modest but spontaneous show of interest began. According to the *Boston Globe,* the *Spray* "and her gallant skipper were visited by hundreds."

Mabel Wagnalls hurried to Newport. "The first name on the *Spray's* visitors' book in the home port was written by the one who always said, 'The *Spray* will come back,'" Slocum wrote near the end of his narrative.

Slocum had carried Mabel's "musical story" around the world. Now he handed it back to her with an inscription.

"A thousand thanks! Good wishes are prayers, heard by the angels. And so June 28th 1898 the little book, after making the circuit of the earth in the single handed *Spray* returns in good order and condition. And it is handed to the author, only on condition that a copy is put in the *Spray* library in its stead. What ups and down *Miserere* you have had in your round! You have been twice through the Straits of Magellan; once off Cape Horn; you have seen Juan Fernandez, St Helena and many more islands in the sea. The Cape of Good Hope, called also 'The Cape of Storms' you weathered unharmed. Again you have lain quietly in your snug box, while the skipper whistled for wind or spent a night on deck in the storm. For weeks and weeks, again little Book, no human voice has stirred the air to vibrate a chord among your leaves, and the only music you heard was the tune of the waves! You saw the lonely atoll in the midst of the sea where the waves lashing and with eternal roar spent their fury on its trembling rim, which never grew less. Spite of the restless sea it grew more! You have been read and re-read by the Captain and the crew of your ship, all rolled into one. Henceforth little Book you will be in smooth seas while benefited old friend may still sail on. Farewell, your story was well told!   J.S.   New Port 28th June, 1898."

Although he had been ignored by the papers, the editor of the prestigious *Century Illustrated Monthly Magazine,* Richard Watson Gilder, sent Slocum a telegram asking if he would be interested in writing up his voyage.* Slocum accepted.

---

* Richard Watson Gilder's younger brother, Joseph B. Gilder, Slocum's friend and correspondent, had been following the *Spray's* progress. So had Clarence Clough Buel, yachtsman and assistant editor of the *Century Magazine.* Both had met Slocum. In an office memorandum, 22 September 1897, Buel suggested to R. W. Gilder that Slocum "might be able to make a lively story of his tens of thousands of miles in a forty-foot sloop."

Mr Editor, Century Magazine:—

Your telegram: Magazine materael I answered this a. m

I have a fund of matter tobesure; but have not myself, had experience in writing magazine articles—I have very decided literary tastes and could enter into such parts as I am able to do with a great deal of energy—

I have made a voyage such as, even, the emperor of Germany could not do and first building his [sic] own ship.

It has been, to me, like reading a book and more interesting as I turned the pages over I know what it all means and I know what *men* have said about it.—When my countrymen come to know about it and have time to think it over they will not be shamed of the Spray

It would be out of place to make ado of it especially at this time; The story will keep. No one short of bone and muscle and pine knots will lower the reccord

The finest work I have done would be called fine even in the navy: as astronomical observations etc

The most interesting and instructive part is never touched by the daily reporters. I am misquoted by them till I am discouraged; for the public stomach *will* sicken—

A *thoughtful* magazine article would square me. If it should have some illustration I might help supply them

I intend, of course, to publish the whole story—in book form—if I can't do better

If you were on the Spray I could show you, Sir, what interest has been taken in her voyage in foreign countries and especially by our British friends;—the highest mark made for the *Spray* being at the Admiralty

Without saying Slocum Slocum all the time—that I do not care for I know that the whole story will be hard to beat—My ship, esentially mine, is as tight today as the best ship afloat; her pump is dry enough for matchwood; not wormed not worn, my ship is as good or better than she was the day I launched her and I myself, I am ten years younger than I was the day I fell the first tree for the construction of my bark. . . .

I am waiting at Newport for the fog to lift, when I sail for New Bedford. It may be clear tomorry or it may be thick for several days and keep me here

After going to N.B. and perhaps Boston I expect to come to your great port—

I could in the mean time come on by train myself if it were a matter of any importance in time etc

Thanking you for your thought of the Spray

I am yours very truly
Joshua Slocum

This letter evidently crossed one from Richard Watson Gilder. The editor of the *Century* apparently wanted to know how much of his story Slocum had already published and what, if anything, there was to the rumor of diamonds arriving on board the *Spray*. On 1 July, still in Newport, Slocum wrote Gilder another long and emotional letter.

Dear Mr Gilder: Your kind letter, partly answered by my letter of yesterday: I beg further to say that I have not written for publication more than one or two short letters to the World (N.Y.), these I discontinued for my own reasons long ago *

There were indeed features of my trip striking enough to interest anybody. It would take the pen of a poet to tell some of the voyage— That of course is beyond me! . . .

I have many photos, some never before used. My best views (some 300) are lantern slides which *will* be called first class in New York or London.

My commercial venture: If my countrymen have hinted at diamonds coming in on the Spray, it is hardly fare of them to do that   I had but $1.50 when I began to build my ship I hadnnt much to trade one or even for luxuries for the cabin for a long time

I thouth of bringing one diamond from Kimberly just to flash at the Goddess of Liberty as we sail up your harbor—the Spray and I; but I did not do even that had I brought it I would have told the Customs of it   I brought away their gold instead; To this I know there is no objection, on any hand

From Johannesburg also I brought gold enough to pay the old debts I made when I owned and sailed the bigger ship

My countrymen shall not be shamed by my commercial transactions nor by the company I keep   My vessel has in a cargo, tobesure, but clean open and above board.

I tried to make myself believe that I was sailing for the dollars I

* Slocum forgot or chose not to mention his travel letters to the *Boston Globe*.

should make in trading, In this way I do make a dollar perhaps as much as Captains make ordinarily but the love of adventure has been, after all a potent factor to cary me beyond—This latter may not appeal to the hearts of my countrymen so much as the dollars and cents; These too I obtained!

Have any of your merchant captains accomplished more—with such limited resources?

I claim only to be one of the poorest of American sailors and having nothing else to do, made a voyage! I am not a dime museum navigator: It will take a man to do the little that even I have done   I am not a bold brave man at all   Some things I found hard to tackle the Young Ladies College, for instance, at the Garden Colony * but I soon found that people wanted to help me   They wanted to laugh—not cry I managed invariably to keep my audiences from falling asleep

I should be pleased to see Mr Gilder and friends at my "show" in New York when I come round to it, but I can not advise it

Mr A W Wagnalls of Funk and Wagnalls knows me very well I daresay you meet Mr W now and then

Thanking you for kind expressions

> I am very sincerely yours
> Joshua Slocum
> The Spray

Two days later Slocum left Newport and sailed for New Bedford and Fairhaven. "The *Spray* was not quite satisfied till I sailed her around to her birthplace, Fairhaven, Massachusetts, farther along," he wrote in the closing paragraphs of *Sailing Alone Around the World*. "I had myself a desire to return to the place of the very beginning whence I had, as I have said, renewed my age. So on July 3, with a fair wind, she waltzed beautifully round the coast and up the Acushnet River to Fairhaven, where I secured her to the cedar spile driven in the bank to hold her when she was launched. I could bring her no nearer home."

Soon after Slocum arrived in Fairhaven he received a visit from Victor and Garfield. The former mate was now 26; Garfield, 15. Victor wrote that his father greeted him, "Vic, you could have done it, but you would not be the first."

Local reporters went aboard. Though some were appreciative

---

* At the Garden Colony, Durban, Slocum "visited many public schools," he wrote in *Sailing Alone*.

—one described the trip as "the most remarkable voyage ever attempted by any navigator"—Slocum, after tossing them his scrapbooks filled with clippings from foreign papers, seemed more interested in talking of what he would do, rather than what he had done. "I am prepared to pay all my bills with the legal rate of interest . . ." he said, according to the *New Bedford Standard*. Then, speaking of the voyage, he added that it "isn't finished yet by any means . . . I intend to go to London before long." From the beginning, Slocum enjoyed greater favor and recognition in England than here.

Almost from the minute the voyage ended, Slocum felt desperately idle and unemployed. The Spanish-American war inflamed his desire for action. "I burn to be of some use now of all times," he announced in a public letter to friends and creditors in New Bedford. "I spent the best of my life in the Philippine islands, China and Japan. . . . I am not fanatically suffering for a fight, but I am longing to be useful. Does Mr. McKinley want pilots for the Philippines and Guam?"

Slocum's routine in New Bedford was much the same as in any port. He rested, refitted his boat, and lectured. Lecturing had become his main source of income. He wanted to go on to London but no offer came from that direction. Looking for business, he went to New York. Hettie accompanied him. They found rooms in the city, "on a crosstown street on the lower West side," Garfield recalled in a letter to me. On 5 August, *The New York Times* noted Slocum's arrival.

There was the offer from the *Century* but writing was not Captain Slocum's first choice of occupation. The idea of a college ship mentioned more than a year before in the letter to Joseph B. Gilder, written from Keeling Cocos, occupied his mind. Such a ship would meet his requirements. It might bring a livelihood but in any case would provide a command.

He explained the scheme before "a few friends," foregathered in a room in Carnegie Hall, on the evening of 30 October. He proposed the building of a vessel patterned on a fine clipper ship, "with some improvements." She was to accommodate 300 student-passengers for a two-year cruise of the world, the time to be spent in study, work, and recreation. The object was to train young men as navigators "capable of handling and directing sailing and steamships including men-of-war." He himself would teach nautical astronomy. Others would give instruction in seamanship, and engineering—and also in some of the liberal arts.

Slocum may have got the germ of the idea from the U.S. Coast Guard's floating academy, the bark *Salmon P. Chase,* which for many years was based at New Bedford. She had been built as a school-ship, and was in commission till 1907. But the captain's concept of a college ship went beyond the usual school-ship education.

There were to be advantages and attractions besides the strictly nautical ones. The student-passenger might, if he preferred, take the courses offered in literature, "and other of the higher branches." Also, the cruise was not to be for men only. The captain had not changed his views since the days when he wanted Virginia on board. In fact, he said he would have no part in his own project, "if women could not be included in its benefits."

Nothing came of this plan.

22

*I will only say
that I have endeavored
to tell just the story
of the adventure itself*

Finding nothing to do in New York, Slocum and Hettie returned to East Boston. At 57 West Eagle Street, where they doubled up for the winter with Odessa Elliott, one of Hettie's sisters, Slocum began writing. On 30 January 1899, he wrote Buel, the assistant editor, "This is to report the *Spray:* My 'type-writer' and I are working along around Cape Horn now and will soon have some work ready to submit. . . ."

When spring came Slocum sailed back to New York where he tied up in South Brooklyn. He worked in the cabin where five years earlier he had written *Voyage of the Destroyer.* Mabel Wagnalls lived in New York. She spurred him on and, at his request, wrote a eulogizing preface—never used and long since lost. By early summer, Slocum delivered the manuscript to his publisher, then sailed for the island of Martha's Vineyard where a number of relatives lived. From Cottage City in the Town of Oak Bluffs, Massachusetts, 23 July 1899, he wrote R. U. Johnson, the *Century Magazine's* associate editor.

Dear Mr Johnson:
    Your kind note of the 5th was forwarded. . . .
    I myself upon reading my M.S., in cooler blood, wondered how I could have made some of the points so obscure
    Some I made clearer   Will you please send the proofs of the second article to Cottage City? I will be here for some days—It is a charming place.

I believe I did not revise from Torres Straits on to the finish. . . .

I think the artist is doing well; And I am delighted with every touch of the editors pen My reading has been sound and my judgment should be good—I know a good thing when I see it!

Slocum also wrote the same day to R. W. Gilder, the editor-in-chief. He said that Mabel, whom he called "very talented," wanted to review his narrative. He explained that her parents were "ambitious for their daughter to make a great name in letters." He asked Gilder to see Mabel if she should call. Gilder handed Slocum's letter to his associate Johnson who in turn scribbled across the top, "Of course we can't let her review the text now." By the word now he seems to have meant, never.

Five days later, still at Cottage City, Slocum wrote Johnson again.

. . . I have a copy of the MS and will do as you wish in boiling down from Rodriquez as far as I may be able

Mr Johnson I dare say has slaughtered, judiciously and liberally up to that point

I will be not farther away than Nantucket, for the next two weeks. . . .

If you will be so kind as to send me proofs as they come along I will give them all attention

I am most anxious to see a clear story appear in both Magazine and book with no superfluous matter

I have tried the editors patience, I dare say

I think I may be able to give the matter for the book many a touch which shall, when all will have been done, make it not the worst marine story in the world

But I find I must come to anchor and make a business of it if I hope to revise intelligently at all

Magazine work, as you must know is intirely new to me, the great Century being the first I ever tackled

Be patient with me still. . . .

And a few days later from "Spray Cottage City Mass," Slocum wrote Buel.

. . . I am glad that my poor MS fell into good hands: In the Century it will appear far different to the ten fathoms of autograph which I first submitted to Mr Buel—how patient Century Editors have been!

I appreciate every touch of the pen given to my poor story Mr Johnson knows that I value also his exceedingly nice way of paying an old sailor a high compliment. Altogether, and best of all, I see my ship coming in under full sail freighted to the loadline

Fair wind to the Century and may the weather clew of your own mainsail be kept hauled up. . . .

This letter to Buel was signed, Josh Slocum. Slocum and his editors seemed to work well together. Sometimes the author when answering the publisher's questions, scribbled his replies on the letter received.

Aug 8 99

Dear Capt Slocum:

When you shortened the rig of the Spray in Buenos Aires did you take in a topmast, or did you shorten the mast?

(Topmast was taken down at Yarmouth N.S.)

(Shortened mast 7 feet, bowsprit 5 feet at BA)

(Yes)

At the same time you shortened the bowsprit. Did you also shorten the boom, and to what extent?

(Shortened the boom inboard 4 ft at Pernambuco)

(Shortened the outboard 4 ft at Port Angosto)

At Port Angosto you put on the jigger. Did you shorten the boom again so as to bring it inboard?

(Yes at the outer end)

And did you *then* put on the stern brace to support the jigger? (No)

If that circular brace was put there earlier, when, where and why was it added to the Spray? (Put on stern brace at Rio to be ready for the mast.)

In the enclosed picture—the encounter with the great wave—the brace is shown—(It was there then) and the boom is as short as when she was yawl-rigged. (It should be four feet over the stern)

Isn't this all a mistake? When you see an error in a picture we want you to speak up—"and spoke it loud."

It was a pleasure to get your letter this morning.

Yours truly
/s/　C C Buel
Assistant Ed

(Oddly enough Mr. Buel: I was just rounding off some swearing about the *Northern Light* picture when your letter was handed to me. . . .)

In his next letter, undated, Slocum enlarged on some of his replies.

I should have mentioned that the jigger-mast which I shipped at Port Angosto was taken on board while at St Marys Bay where I found it among drift-wood on the beach It was one of those "hardy Spruce" saplings.

The boom projected over the stern till the jigger mast was stepped sufficient of the outer end, and then sawd off to allow it to swing clear—

This same boom was previously broken in the gale off the coast of Morocco and was fished then, near the mainmast, The short broken end was removed at Pernambuco and the jaws refitted this brought the boom in about four feet but left some four feet still projecting over the stern until she was refitted as before stated, at Port Angosto. It seems difficult—allmost impossible—to get marine pictures done nearely right

The Ship N.L. is made too stiff and is hogged, her stern droops, but in the degenerate state of our marine thes matters have been overlooked. The man who revives interest will deserve our prayers

Long afterwards, 1967, Constance Buel Burnett, Buel's daughter, in a letter to *The Christian Science Monitor,* said, "My father . . . took a prominent part in the publication of . . . Joshua Slocum's own account of his solitary cruise. Himself an enthusiastic sailor, my father invited Joshua Slocum to anchor the *Spray* in the Long Island Sound waters in front of our summer home, and stay awhile. . . . My recollections of the *Spray* are vivid, especially the smell of the cabin, pungent with the odor of tarred ropes and the salty mildew a boat collects while sailing the seven seas."

Alice C. Longaker, who summered with her family at Lagoon Heights, Martha's Vineyard, was thirteen when Slocum showed up there in 1899. "We saw him many-times walk back and forth in front of our cottage on his way to and from his sisters' home," she wrote me. "One of the more memorable facts about his physical being was the set of his head. I think he'd both literally and in his mind's eye had to telescope his neck in order to duck back and forth, in and out of the galley or cabin so often that it became simpler just to wear his head close to his shoulders. I saw him off and on for a number of years. . . . I cannot remember seeing him ever in any but a blue serge suit."

Further work on the text remained to be done but the time was summer, and Cottage City was a summer resort. Slocum found the place distracting. From Woods Hole, 12 August, he wrote Johnson again.

In order to get onto the work of revising the story from Rodrigues on, badly needed, I sailed from Cottage City altogather—yesterday

About three quarters of the matter is greatly improved by the going over I will send that and other matter along tomorrow or next day

I write this to assure you that I am not neglecting this interest

I can do the work better away where it is quiet

I have not yet seen the galley proof of part II Magazine

To answer some questions in part III I had to refer to my logbook. . . .

Two days later, from Fairhaven, Slocum wrote Johnson again.

I send with this MS copy from Rodriguez on to the finish of the voyage with what improvements I could make

I will very gladly pay for retypewriting it that the editor may have a clearer swing at it

I fear that I have not condensed as much as you wished; but have cut some paragraphs

I find it rather difficult to condense the variety of experiences while sailing free over the smooth sea from Good Hope. It was all ripple ripple However the editor will know how to slaughter my pet so as to keep the matter down to at least five installments But it is a rule, at Lloyds, that one cannot have too much of a good thing

As publication time approached, Mabel and the preface she had written were on Slocum's mind. Mabel's part had become a complication. From Fairhaven, 18 August, Slocum wrote Buel.

A lady in your city is giving me the very duce over a preface which evidently has been mislaid, and I think in the Century office at that!

I think I handed it to Mr Buel when I first landed that great batch
of round-about stuff. I can understand how a smaller paper ever so
important might get lost among the driftwood   However I send now,
the original—the other was a typewritten copy—I thought at one time,
that it would be a great lift to my poor book, if it ever got afloat;
the editors may think intirely different. . . . "Mabel Wagnalls" I think
is a good writer, clever and strong: In the case of the preface, perhaps
too strong   One should be careful to not raise a debate and to be over
praised is worse than all. I would rather be paired down in the
Century Brain Department than go out to the merciless world with a
large head. But the dear lady is broken hearted!

I shall never be able to make her believe, kind soul, that on top
of the Century send off: "Defoe like" etc nothing more could be
said. . . .

I feel very sure that Mr Buel will get me out of the difficulty that
will come if the preface is not used: May I suggest without being
oficious, that our really gifted friend write a story of adventure? I'll
go to Iceland or the North Pole if no other subject can be found to
write about—and be glad of the chance—

While Slocum was cruising in Buzzards Bay, the postman did
not know where to knock to deliver proof. From Onset, Massachusetts, 25 August, Slocum sent Buel a note.

It was through the oversight of the postman at Cottage City that
I did not get the proofs

They forwarded me all the letters for all the Slocums and their
wives, out of heaven, a great batch, and my own I heard of only an
hour before I received these sheets yesterday. . . . Mrs S is with me
on the Spray. . . .

From the empty clamshells of a watering place one can expect no
better that I got at Cottage City. Please excuse me

From Fairhaven, Slocum sent Johnson a note praising one of
his illustrators. "Mr Fogarty is a careful worker   he has sketched
the spot the *Spray* returned to exactly as it appeares: the old stake
she tied up to and all."

Sailing Alone Around the World, illustrated by Thomas Fogarty
and George Varian, appeared in the *Century Illustrated Monthly
Magazine,* beginning in September 1899 and continuing through

March 1900. By the time the third installment came out, Slocum and Hettie were back in East Boston, this time sharing quarters at 184 Princeton Street with another of Hettie's sisters, Beatrice Elliott Ferguson. Slocum wrote Buel, 30 October, "I am very proud of the company the *Spray* is in: Mark Twain's contribution in November Century is the best thing he has ever done in his long life of good work. . . . I congratulate the Century and myself."

Mark Twain's contribution, *My Debut as a Literary Person,* had special appeal for Slocum. It told how Clemens, when a young journalist for the *Sacramento Union*—journalism had appealed to Slocum, too—had covered the story of the survivors of the clipper ship *Hornet* which burned at sea in 1866.

Slocum did not stop long with Hettie and Beatrice. Early November found him back in New York at the six-story United States Hotel near the East River waterfront, on Fulton Street between Water and Pearl, a short walk from the pier where the *Northern Light* had docked years before. While *Sailing Alone* was appearing in serial form, Slocum made further revisions for the forthcoming book. The *Spray*, meanwhile, lay at a pier in Brooklyn.

Though *The New York Times* let Slocum's trip go unnoticed, his story unfolding month by month in the *Century*, beguiled the anonymous columnist who wrote "Topics of the Times." What amazed and mystified him was not that one man alone should circumnavigate the earth in a sailing boat of his own construction, but that he should have sailed in the manner he said he did. Could he really have lashed the helm and slept? Could the *Spray* have steered herself, so to speak?

"Topics of the Times," 7 November 1899, said, "Interesting as undoubtedly are the articles in which Capt. JOSHUA SLOCUM is telling . . . of his voyage . . . there is lacking from them one thing the absence of which is a sore trial to the temper—and a somewhat severe trial to the credulity—of all of us who have or pretend a knowledge of matters nautical. Capt. Slocum repeatedly asserts that the *Spray* was so rigged that she both could and would steer herself, or, to paraphrase his statements more explicitly, that he could so arrange his sails and so lash his rudder that his boat would keep on her course all night while her . . . Captain . . . slept quietly in his cabin. The tale is painfully hard to believe . . . we won't say that the Captain has been treating the truth with irreverence, or even that he is honestly mistaken as to the *Spray's* intelligence. We will keep within a safe regret that he didn't reveal how the apparent miracle was performed. Queer things have been and will be done at sea. . . ."

Slocum replied the next day, and on 11 November the *Times* published his letter, datelined Sloop *Spray*.

I am honored by a criticism from an old salt . . . It is possible that things occured on the voyage of the *Spray* inexplicable to some mariners, even of vast experience, and I can only regret not having met them before the articles . . . were written so that I might have taken them on a sail in the *Spray* to demonstrate her prowess. As the matter stands, it is now out of my power to further elucidate. . . .

This unpretentious sloop, built by one pair of hands, after circum-navigating the globe, is sound and snug and tight. She does not leak a drop. This would be called a great story by some; nevertheless it is a hard fact.

The story of the voyage is constructed on the same seaworthy lines; that is, it remains waterproof which your navigating officer will discover, I trust, if only he exercise to the end that patience necessary on a voyage around the world.

Came the rebuttal. The columnist wrote he was "ready to believe almost anything about a ship or a boat, but belief and readiness to believe are not quite equivalent, and unfortunately, Capt. Slocum is not in a demonstrative or explanatory mood."

Slocum did not deign a reply. "The *Times* joker I can stow any time in my waistcoat pocket," he wrote Buel.

The *Times's* last word on the subject was not spoken till 6 March 1900, after the final installment of *Sailing Alone* had appeared: "A note at the end of Capt. JOSHUA SLOCUM's narrative . . . promised, or seemed to promise . . . a supplementary article explaining how the Captain taught the *Spray* the difficult art of steering herself. That he really had accomplished this mar-vellous educational feat was asserted many times. . . . Capt. SLOCUM declares that he sailed from Thursday Island to the Keeling Cocos, 2,700 miles, in 23 days, and in all that time stood at the wheel not more than an hour.* We have no inclination to question the accuracy of his figures, but, even with the most favorable conditions of wind and sea, did the *Spray*, when left to her own devices, constantly keep on her course, as that phrase is commonly understood, or did she reach her destination along a zig-zag path, falling off and coming up as her head sails and those aft alternately got the better of each other? If the latter suggestion is true, how much simpler the Captain's explanation might have been made."

The *Spray* became, and remains to this day, a controversial subject. Properly set on her course, however, she could, under various circumstances, hold it, unaided by anyone at the wheel. This was confirmed by several friends who subsequently sailed with Slocum.

Though the *Spray's* steering qualities are no longer questioned, her model and rig still provoke discussion. There are those who think that Slocum succeeded, not because of the *Spray*, but in spite of her. A writer for one of the yachting magazines warned yachtsmen against building copies of the sloop. He called her "the worst possible boat for anyone, and especially anyone lacking the experience and resourcefulness of Slocum, to take off soundings." The *Spray* has been compared to a Cape Cod cat-boat; while extremely stiff initially, if ever heeled beyond a critical point, she would flop over as inevitably as the platter which she resembled.

Whatever the virtues or defects of a boat like the *Spray*, she was Slocum's boat. L. Francis Herreshoff, son of the famous yacht designer, Captain Nat Herreshoff, wrote me, "My father did not think much of the *Spray* but he had great admiration for Captain Slocum's ability to go around the world in such a poor vessel."

As recently as April 1965, the *National Fisherman*, Camden, Maine, published a letter from a Swede who wanted to build another *Spray*. The same issue included a letter advising against it, written by Howard I. Chapelle, Curator in Charge, Division of Transportation, Smithsonian Institution. "There is no authentic lines plan of *Spray* and she was not an ideal vessel for long ocean

---

* Concerning this leg of the voyage, Slocum wrote that he did not spend "more than three hours at the helm, including the time occupied in beating into Keeling harbor." (*Sailing Alone*, Chapter XVI.) W.T.

voyages—unless Slocum was aboard. This is in spite of the fact that she eventually drowned him," Chapelle wrote.

"From reports of yachtsmen and one naval architect who visited her," Chapelle continued, "the *Spray* was a poor job, badly framed and fastened. Slocum was not a boat carpenter, of course. . . . It is sheer ignorance to tout this damned bucket as a 'splendid ship.' . . . How anyone of experience and judgment can be brought to accept *Spray* as the acme of all designs for an ocean voyage I do not understand. . . . The old man was a prime seaman to stay on top, with her, as long as he did."

Kenneth E. Slack of Australia, Vice Commodore of the Slocum Society Sailing Club, who wrote an entire book, *In the Wake of the Spray,* extolling the *Spray,* replied to Mr. Chapelle (*National Fisherman,* July 1965). "As an ardent student of the *Spray* for the past fifteen years, I would like to come to her defense in the face of charges as misinformed as they are exaggerated. . . . As Mr. Chapelle should know, there is no absolute criterion of what constitutes an *ideal* vessel for long ocean voyages; even expert sailors and architects disagree. Surely the *Spray's* behavior on her world voyage and that of the two dozen odd copies and modifications built and sailed extensively since by men far less skilled than Slocum would show that her seaworthiness and safety were ample."

To which Chapelle answered, "So far as the 'facts' about *Spray* are concerned, I wish to remind Mr. Slack that Slocum was lost in her and that none (so far as I know) of the owners of 'modifications' or 'replicas' have apparently duplicated Slocum's voyages. . . . The record also shows that luck, and the little cherub aloft, has allowed some voyagers to do amazing things. . . . Crossings in the most unsuitable craft have led some to believe, apparently, that anything in the way of a boat will serve for a crossing. However, we do not hear, usually, of the people who do not make it. . . . The sea is a beautiful thing, at peace, but in the fury of a storm it has a terrible power and a merciless attack on a weak boat. . . . As a few survivors can testify, the sea has capsized boats up to the size of *Spray* end-over-end, so there are obviously conditions where no boat, under 60' or 70' length is safe and even vessels above this range of size are lost."

Thanks to serious work by Chapelle and Slack, to the testimony of many who saw the *Spray,* and to those who photographed her, a great deal is known about the boat; everything except how Slocum handled her—what mattered most.

23

*but above all
to be taken into account
were some years of schooling,
where I studied with diligence
Neptune's laws*

Sailing Alone Around the World, dedicated "To the one who said: 'The *Spray* will come back,'" appeared in book form 24 March 1900. Bound in navy-blue cloth embossed with an anchor and sea horses, 294 pages of heavy stock topped with gilding, it sold for $2. Later printings scrimped stock, margins and binding.*

The illustrations by Thomas Fogarty (1873–1938) and George Edmund Varian (1865–1923) which embellished the serialization, reappeared in the book. Fogarty, who did most of the drawings, was born in New York, studied at the Art Students League, taught illustration and became a leading illustrator of his day. None of the many books he illustrated, however, is as read today as Slocum's. Varian, born in Liverpool, England, studied at the

* The Century and successor companies printed all told 27,760 copies in 17 printings and kept *Sailing Alone* in print until 1948. In the 1930s, Blue Ribbon Books issued 16,200 copies of a lower-priced reprint. Rights in the book, which in 1951 reverted to the estate of Joshua Slocum, were subsequently assigned to Sheridan House, Inc. In 1954, Sheridan House put out an edition of *Sailing Alone* with a preface by myself. Two years later the copyright expired and the book went into the public domain. Dover Publications re-issued it in soft cover that year. *The Voyages of Joshua Slocum* (Rutgers University Press), Slocum's three books in one volume, collected and introduced by myself, was published in 1958. Collier Books published a paperback of *Sailing Alone* and *Voyage of the Liberdade* edited by myself in 1962.

Brooklyn Art Guild as well as the Art Students League, and did most of his work for *McClure's Magazine.* Some illustrations distort the writing, others enhance it. Slocum was fortunate in his illustrators. Their work, like his, has met the test of the years.

The Century Company promoted *Sailing Alone* with a four-page illustrated flyer quoting reviews from various papers. First place went to Sir Edwin Arnold (1832–1904), British journalist and poet, author of *The Light of Asia.* He said of Slocum's narrative, "The most extraordinary book, in its way, ever published. The adventure itself is by far the most courageous, sustained and successful enterprise of the kind ever undertaken by mortal man."

Slocum, promoting his book on his own, got up a one-page broadside on which he gave Mabel Wagnalls pride of place. " 'Round the world alone'—a mighty motto this," she wrote, "and in all the world's history it applies to only one man—Captain Joshua Slocum. Amid solitude and silence, with the keel of his little boat he has traced the great circle—the emblem of eternity." He also gave her a copy of *Sailing Alone* inscribed, "To Mabel Wagnalls who said 'The *Spray* will come back' and who first read the manuscript of the Voyage. With sincere good wishes. Joshua Slocum   New York   April 8, 1900."

Slocum was pleased to find a line drawing portrait of himself—made from a photograph—near the back of the book. He wrote Buel from East Boston.

It is as you say: your artist has made a fine looking man appear to the gaze of all who turn over the pages of Sailing Alone to 235 But for all, his good looks, the skipper of the Spray like his accomplished editors prides himself more on winning ways!

The Spray *herself* appears in the frontispiece one feels while looking at her that one might step onboard there and sail on. . . .

Now that the book was out in the world, Slocum worried; what would the papers say about it? Hardy and tough in many ways, he seems to have been thin-skinned in others. "He was capable of letting his irascible side show up if provocation was given or even suspected," a sympathetic relative wrote me. "One could not hide anything from a mind like his and small slights would rankle and never be forgotten or forgiven." On 17 April, still in East Boston, Slocum wrote Buel.

I expect I'll get fits if the Transcript "goes" for me but the man who gave me the note to the editor has marked the little work in his window: "The best Sea story ever written"! So much for Boston. . . .

A friend introduced me to the editor of the Herald today who had lots of good things to say about the Magazine articles but, as far as I know had not said them beyond his own sanctum. Many think that I will get a house Monday

I'll give Bostonians beans if I dont, I'll give them beans anyhow, if I can

Enclose please find a couple of tickets to my show Monday 23rd.*

Two weeks later, he still was worrying:

I have heard nothing from the critics about my "fine writing" and hope to hear nothing.

If they'll only pass me this time Ill steer clear of like shallows in the future. I beg that the changes may be made in the plates especially on page 12

While I do not pose as a professional writer I should not leave a libel on the American Shipmaster

I was considerably interested in the story at the time of telling it and didn't see the enormous sunken ledges that I see now. . . .

I have not gone critically over this child of the sea but after a cooling off I see at a glance many improvements which I shall be able to make in the text—a touch here and there. Doing so would be no more than the great author of Ivanho did. I wonder if another editions will be wanted wherein I may somewhat retrieve?

There was no need for concern. The reviews were good, few as uninspired as that in the *New York Times*. The *Times* reviewer called the book "full of interest to lovers of adventure."

The *Nautical Gazette* said of Slocum, "His voyage was interest-

---

* The "show" was "A Sea Talk" at Tremont Temple, Boston, 23 April 1900, 8 P.M. It was advertised as illustrated with stereopticon views. Tickets sold from 25¢ to $1. The following day, the *Boston Herald* reported an audience of "several hundred people." A cousin, Mrs. Fannie I. Maclean of Reading, Mass., recalling the captain on that evening, wrote me, "He was in full evening clothes, was very much at ease, and very witty. . . ."

ing; his book is better." *Sailing Alone* was described as "a book of travel by sea that is well nigh perfect of its kind, the work of an artistic and therefore a master hand."

The reviewer for the *New York Mail and Express* found a second reading "even more entertaining than the first, for it revealed many touches overlooked . . . and gave more opportunity to admire the way in which the story is told, as well as the story itself."

The *Nation,* and the *New York Evening Post* used the same review. "Absence of literary finish and florid word-painting sinks into insignificance compared with the overwhelming impression his story conveys of dominant courage and placid self-reliance. . . . With all the attention that was lavished upon him, his sense of humor was not diminished. . . ." The reviewer proposed Slocum for the Hall of Fame which was about to be founded.*

The notice in the *Nation* was read in London by R. B. Marston of Sampson Low, Marston & Co. He obtained the book and wrote Slocum, "I was laid up at home under orders not to read, but I began your book after breakfast, and sailed the whole of the 40,000 and odd miles with you before night, and wished for another 40,000. . . . We are Jules Verne's English publishers. Your fact is stranger than his fiction. . . ."

Sampson Low, Marston & Co. published *Sailing Alone* in the summer of 1900. Sir Edwin Arnold reviewed it in the *Daily Telegraph,* 8 September. "No one, knowing the sea, and following Captain Slocum's narrative, would tolerate any snigger of suspicion, with which ignorant persons ofttimes accost great deeds. . . . The tale is true from first to last, written in a style plain as a marlin-spike, and yet full of touches which show what hidden poetry and passionate love of Nature were in the soul of this 'blue-nose' skipper. . . ."

After starting out with good reviews and a modest but profitable sale—about 7,000 copies in its first year—*Sailing Alone* made headway slowly. Years came when only the interest of yachtsmen kept it in print; among amateur sailors everywhere Slocum's book

---

* The Hall of Fame was established in 1900 on New York University campus. From 1919 to 1937 one of Slocum's editors, R. U. Johnson, served as its Director. Slocum is not among those honored there with memorial busts and tablets.

is scripture. Yet it never could have been only a yachtsman's book because with the passing of time it became a classic.

Sailing Alone Around the World is a book one feels better for having read. A record of its author's beliefs and values, it is a product of his struggle not to let himself down in his own eyes. Stories of loners and bolters are seldom as simple as they seem. Beneath the outwardly amiable witty manner a complicated man emerges, one who lived the divided life—involvement and escape, acquisitiveness and simplicity. By keeping the action in focus, Slocum concealed from his contemporaries the inner form of the book; that while he sailed onward he also moved inward.

J. Duncan Spaeth, who taught American literature at Princeton University, was so struck by Slocum's literary style that he went to Gloucester to see him some time around 1900. Years later, Spaeth wrote me, "I remember seeing an edition of Hakluyt's *Voyages*, well worn and evidently well read . . . on whose style Slocum's own was modeled. . . ." Spaeth recommended *Sailing Alone Around the World* to his students.

I do not see the influence of Hakluyt on Slocum's writing. When asked how he had acquired his style, Slocum replied, "I was not aware that I had any particular style; I certainly never studied to possess one." Understandably. The style, like the experience, was a singular one.

Slocum had no literary theories. A master of sail, spiritually as well as economically displaced, unschooled and isolated in his own time, he was a kind of naive writer with the typical predilection for writing about himself.

By the same token he was a genre writer, the last and greatest of the race of sea captain-writers who flourished in the eighteenth and nineteenth centuries along the New England coast. In my book, *Five Sea Captains*, 1960, I traced that tradition.

There is another element in Slocum's writing, and which also has to do with his early environment and its popular and oral tradition. In the middle of the nineteenth century, a good deal of seventeenth-century English still was spoken by the everyday people of English-Scotch descent in rural Nova Scotia. King James English was a built-in feature of Slocum's language, and it did not come from much reading of the Authorized Version. Indeed, he never spoke of reading the Bible, and there is no indication that he had a copy on the *Spray*. Garfield wrote me that his father sailed without one. Earlier in his career, when as captain of the *Northern Light*, and then the *Aquidneck*, certain of his duties required a Bible, he had borrowed Virginia's.

Slocum was a deeply religious man, but the harshness and narrowness of the religion he saw in his childhood turned him forever against creed, and whatever he thought smacked of cant. A man of his own kind, he had his own way of expressing adoration and wonder.

Since the first publication of *Sailing Alone Around the World*, there have always been some who insisted the book was ghosted. In his letter to the *National Fisherman*, April 1965, Howard I. Chapelle pronounced statements in Slocum's book not his but "his ghostwriter's, for the captain was hardly literate as his letters show."

On the contrary, Slocum's letters reveal his power and talent. They show that as a writer he was a natural. Taken out of school and put to work at age ten, he never learned to spell or punctuate but, as editors and writers know, those details do not matter.

In May 1965, Benjamin Crocker Clough, Professor of Classics, Emeritus, Brown University, wrote me, "Do you think *Sailing Alone Around the World* is the work of a ghost-writer? A card from Capt. S. to me just after the book came out (in reply to a fan letter) does not indicate that he needed one." The card to Professor Clough who was then about 14 and living in his native Vineyard Haven, Massachusetts, was dated 22 July 1902.

My dear Master Clough
    Your post card came to me at Tisbury
    I am always glad to learn that my poor effort gives pleasure to another reader; and I thank you for your courtesy. Your very polite letter will be retained in the *Spray* Library among valued autographs from all over the world

Yours sincerely
Joshua Slocum

In 1903, Charles Scribner's Sons published an abridgment, *Around the World in the Sloop Spray—A* Geographical Reader Describing Captain Slocum's Voyage Around the World by Captain Joshua Slocum. In a preface to the excised version, Slocum characteristically abbreviated the way it happened.

It was my good fortune, a short time ago, to be invited to the School of Pedagogy,* in New York to meet Dr. Edward R. Shaw. Dr. Shaw was in the midst of a lecture when I entered the room, reading from a famous book of the sea † that he had edited for school uses. From this he turned to *Sailing Alone Around the World*, which, to my surprise and delight, he quoted off the reel.

Here I met a large-hearted man at the right moment. He read my mind, or how else could he perceive my desire to see the story of the *Spray's* voyage still more useful?

"With the leave of your publishers," said Dr. Shaw, "I will make the story of the *Spray's* voyage adaptable to school uses. . . . Then we shall have a story of adventure and a lesson in geography all in one. . . ."

In launching the new literary packet I desire to commend it especially to the indulgence of children around and all over the world.

J.S.

Though well intended, and a wonderfully agreeable way to learn geography, the abridgment was pedagogical in the wooden sense of the word, as inferior to the original as its title to the true title. Even so, many people reading it, thought they were reading *Sailing Alone*. That was partly Slocum's doing. He got hold of copies of *Around the World in the Sloop Spray* and sold them without explaining the difference. While to Slocum the writer there were indeed differences, to Slocum the trader the differences did not matter—a book was a book.

* Graduate School of Pedagogy at New York University.
† *Two Years Before the Mast.*

Somewhere in South America? 1895?

An unidentified port, probably South America, 1895.

Strait of Magellan. Columbus Library, Pan American Union.

One of the best pictures of the *Spray* under sail (1897), courtesy of Kenneth
E. Slack of Australia.

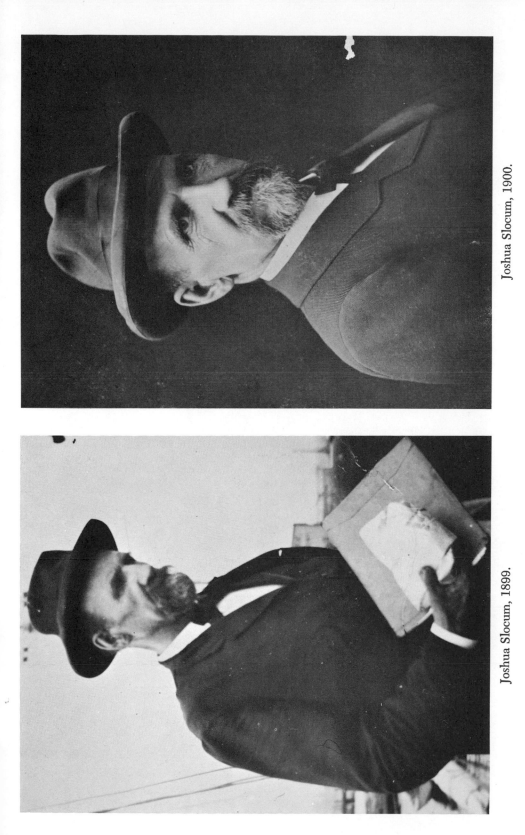

Joshua Slocum, 1900.

Joshua Slocum, 1899.

Salem, Mass., ca. 1900.

On board the *Spray*, 1902. Photo by Clifton Johnson.

On board the *Spray*, 1902. Photo by Clifton Johnson.

187

On board the *Spray*, 1902. Photo by Clifton Johnson.

On board the *Spray*, 1902. Photo by Clifton Johnson.

188

Slocum and Hettie farming, West Tisbury, Mass., 1902. Photo by Clifton Johnson.

Slocum and Hettie, 1902. Photo by Clifton Johnson.

The farmhouse, West Tisbury, Mass., 1902. Photo by Clifton Johnson.

West Tisbury, Mass., 1902. Photo by Clifton Johnson.

190

Slocum at Marion, Mass., 1903.

The *Spray*, Martha's Vineyard, 1904.

The *Spray* in the lagoon at Vineyard Haven, Mass., 1905.

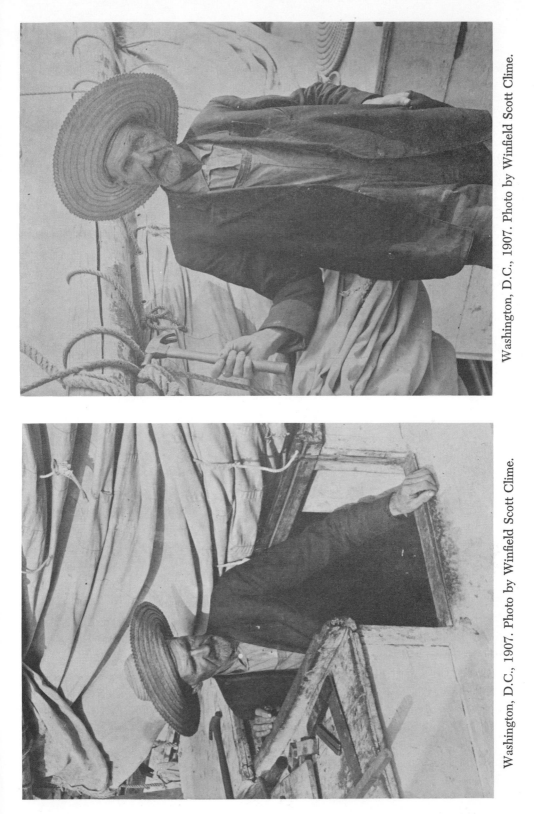

Washington, D.C., 1907. Photo by Winfield Scott Clime.

Washington, D.C., 1907. Photo by Winfield Scott Clime.

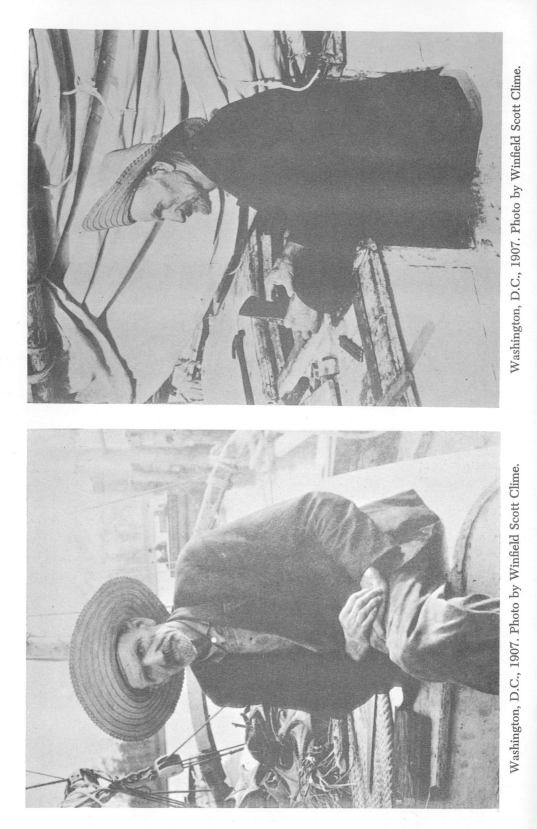

Washington, D.C., 1907. Photo by Winfield Scott Clime.

Washington, D.C., 1907. Photo by Winfield Scott Clime.

194

Washington, D.C., 1907. Photo by Winfield Scott Clime.

In New England waters, ca. 1905.

Branford, Conn., 1907. Note change of sail plan.

Washington, D.C., 1907. Photo by Percy E. Budlong.

Hauled out, Miami, Florida, 1908. Photo by Vincent Gilpin.

Hettie with Walter Teller, West Tisbury, Mass., 1952.

Part IV

24

with such as love sailing,
mother-wit is the best teacher,
after experience

The ever-recurring problem confronting the entrepreneur and free lance is what to do next. Slocum proposed taking the *Spray* to Paris for the Universal Exhibition of 1900 but was turned down. Restless and at loose ends, by spring of that year, he was desperate for something to do. He even considered selling the *Spray* in order to finance a new adventure. From East Boston, 30 March 1900, he wrote his friend Buel.

I hope that the Century will not forget me and the Iceland trip! It may not be of absorbing interest—but I have a voyage in mind that will fasten itself upon all classes of readers and to realize that voyage I am looking to the disposal, first, of the *Spray;* people buy things rare in history   someone may buy my old boat and so help me into my submarine explorer.

The plan for underwater exploration—whatever it was—did not take shape. The *Spray,* instead of being sold, spent another winter moored in South Brooklyn. While Garfield minded the boat, Slocum and Hettie occupied rooms in New York at 11 East 17th Street. Slocum's search for action became more bizarre. He was ready to try any form of the unknown, from diving to flying. While he had been away on the voyage around, Samuel Pierpont Langley had launched the first sustained free flights of power-propelled heavier-than-air machines. Though the flights were unmanned, they attracted world-wide excitement. Slocum wrote an old acquaintance who was also a colleague of Langley's at the Smithsonian Institution, 27 February 1901.

Dear Professor Mason *

I am sending by this post, a book of some account of a voyage alone. I am not the old fossil that some take me for and I am not for old ideas when new are better

I was hoping that Professor Langly or some one else would have launched a successful flying ship before this and that I could have a second mates position on it to soar

I felt sure that when you have time to scan my poor story you will find that I consider the human mind above all else that we know of in this world. You will see that at any rate I could trust even my own poor head to find my way about independent of the machine we call chronometer. I sailed scientiffically, too. I was in touch with Nature as few have ever been. I was aware of it all the time and had never a doubt of the outcome of my voyage

With great respect
Joshua Slocum

Garfield, living on the sloop, saw little of Slocum that winter. "Father did not come on board the *Spray* much," he wrote me, "did not come to inquire if I needed any food or if he could help me; was a mystery to me and will be to my dying day. I assume that he and Hettie did not pull on the same rope. Hettie was cool towards me. Father acted as though he wanted to be alone. One day he came and told me that we would cast off and get underweigh for Buffalo in the spring of 1901. He said the Pan-American Exposition would pay him for the privilege of exhibiting the *Spray*."

So instead of heading for London or Paris or Iceland, or embarking on submarine or airborne adventure, Slocum made preparations for a voyage to Buffalo. Garfield wrote me several letters about it. Slocum bought a 1½ horsepower marine engine, comparable to the smallest present-day outboard motor, and a clinker-built lifeboat. He had the boat fitted to the engine and Garfield instructed in operating the latter. The engine-driven lifeboat was to tow the *Spray* up the Hudson River to Troy, thence

* Otis Tufton Mason (1838–1908) was curator of ethnology at the Smithsonian Institution. In 1902, he became head curator of anthropology.

to Buffalo via the Erie Canal; Garfield to run the improvised tug while Slocum managed the *Spray*.

Slocum, Hettie and Garfield set off on the inland voyage. "Father told me to hug the shore and he steered near the shore because the current running upstream helped. Every night we tied up to whatever we could find."

The Hudson, in its lower course, is a tidal river. From Albany to New York Bay, 145 miles away, the fall is only five feet. At Albany, reporters went aboard the *Spray*. Garfield said that at this time his father did not like reporters, in fact, "hated publicity." Though in his earlier years Slocum had enjoyed, by and large, a good press, there was a tendency now to ridicule him. Disrespectful reporting hurt his pride and added to his frustration.

Six miles above Albany, at Troy, the two masts of the *Spray* were unstepped and lashed on deck. On entering the Erie Canal, Slocum remarked to Garfield, "This is the roughest water I ever sailed on." Garfield added that when they reached Buffalo, all hands were well, no one seasick. He said that the *Spray* attracted a great deal of notice, both along the way and when placed on exhibition.

The Pan-American Exposition opened 1 May and ran till 2 November. It was held in Delaware Park, a 365-acre tract, including a 46-acre lake, and adjoining a tributary of the Niagara River. To reach the park lake, called Gala Water, the *Spray* had to be hauled out and raised in a sling which the captain devised from a hawser, loaded onto a dray drawn by four horses (Garfield on board all the while), and finally launched in the lake by means of a cradle Slocum built on the spot. There she remained six months while tourists were urged "to shake hands with the gallant captain, a man of stout heart and steady nerve, a veteran of the salt seas, and a man of mighty soul and character."

While the captain rode at anchor between the Triumphal Bridge and the dazzling Electric Tower with its thousands of lights, forty-two Indian tribes were whooping it up in the Stadium. Beneath the dome of the Temple of Music, the band pounded out the Latin-American rhythms of Victor Herbert's *Pan Americana*. On the Midway, sightseers gaped at fur-clad Eskimos in imitation ice igloos, South Sea Islanders in native dress, South American hidalgos, hula-hula dancers, large-headed dwarfs, the infant incubator, and Chicquita, The Human Doll. There were other attractions: A Trip to the Moon, or the Streets of Mexico and spurious bull-fighting; the Old Plantation with banjo-strumming singers, the Hawaiian Village, the Beautiful Orient, the Scenic Railway, the Magic House of Mystery, the Wild Animal Show, and Alt Nuremberg. Scenes of the Spanish-American War were re-enacted. U.S. Cavalry Troops reproduced Custer's Last Charge. There was an Indian who impersonated Geronimo, the Apache chief; a lady who interpreted Cleopatra.

Slocum had only himself and the boat, and Hettie and Garfield to exhibit. He answered the visitors' questions, and autographed and sold his books: *Sailing Alone*, $2; *Voyage of the Liberdade*— he still had a few copies—$1; and a new item—*Sloop Spray Souvenir*, 25 cents.

Sloop Spray Souvenir, Arranged and Supplied with Notes by Henrietta E. Slocum, was a 48-page paperbound booklet, 4 x 6 inches in size. Copyright 1901 by Joshua Slocum, it was obviously the work of his hand, though he used Hettie's name.

"A collection of reviews of the *Spray's* famous voyage around the world, from leading journals, with something tangible of the *Spray* herself—namely, a piece of her original mainsail, which was torn, beyond repair, in the gale off Cape Horn, 4th to 8th of March, 1896,—a fierce tempest!

"Admiring friends of the *Spray*, visiting her with jackknives, first and last, by their keen appreciation of souvenirs, suggested the preparation of this memento. . . ."

Tipped in opposite the title page of *Sloop Spray Souvenir* was a bit of stained heavy canvas, a swatch from the sails replaced in Australia but still held onto. The *Souvenir*, very rare, is remarkably personal; to thumb and finger the scrap of sail, almost awesome.

Garfield told me the names of those who visited the *Spray* filled three volumes, among them President McKinley, who was assassinated on the Exposition grounds.

Slocum left Buffalo some time that autumn. Since Garfield had taken a job, Slocum sold the lifeboat and engine. He would have to concoct a new means for towing the *Spray* to salt water. A newspaper account of his departure read, "Horse is Capt. Slocum's Sail / Navigator of the *Spray* Weighs Anchor and Sets Off Down the Raging Erie Canal. / Is Going to be a Farmer / Hand Which Held the Tiller is Soon to Hold the Plow—Satisfied With His Exposition Experience."

"With an old work horse for a sail, the *Spray* sailed down the Erie Canal yesterday afternoon in the general direction of the Hudson River. Capt. Joshua Slocum was standing on the deck, bidding a farewell to Buffalo and all that is left of the Exposition. . . .

"No Whistling For a Breeze.

" 'You see,' explained the captain, 'it don't make much difference which way the wind blows we get there just the same. No, I didn't have the horse sharp shod. The canal don't go over many hills between here and the Hudson.'

"About the time the horse will be all in the good sloop will reach Troy, then Capt. Slocum, thoughtful man that he is, will entice the horse aboard, set real sail and glide down the Hudson and through the Sound as far as Martha's Vineyard.

"The *Spray* has lain in the Erie Canal at the foot of Ferry Street since the night that the waiter turned the hose on the crowds at Pabst's on the Midway.

"The horse that furnished the motive power to run the sloop down the canal will furnish the power to run a plow on the captain's farm in Martha's Vineyard. The hand that steered the tiller of the *Spray* will steer the plow; the voice that refused to allow a woman to accompany him across the Atlantic will say 'gee-up' to the horse, when it comes plowin' time. . . .

" 'Yes,' concluded he as the sloop pulled away from Ferry Street, 'I got two-thirds of the money owed me by the Exposition Company. I met fine people, was treated well, and considering everything, am satisfied.' "

Garfield's last word on the Pan-American was, "I wonder how father steered the horse."

25

beware of reefs day or night,
or, remaining on the land,
be wary still

With his Pan-American Exposition money, and earnings from lecturing and writing, Slocum was able to buy what he thought he wanted—certainly what Hettie wanted—a house of their own. He had already written Buel, "The Century did well by me. . . . No one knows how much I have been paid When they ask me I say 'double the amount agread upon'—which is so—They say 'how much is that?' I say enough to buy me a house—which is also true and as good a house too I could wish to live in All the old women will be sending in sea stories and be looking for houses on the Av when they hear of my amazing success (financial). . . ."

Garfield wrote me his father had said that if he settled down, it would be in the Hawaiian Islands; he liked the climate. When the time came, however, he chose a New England island, Martha's Vineyard, where some of his sisters and a brother lived, and where he was not a stranger.

The *Vineyard Gazette,* 1 March 1902, reported, "Capt. Slocum who has the fame of going around the world in a sail boat has purchased the residence and lot formerly owned by the late John Manter. Also other land of Samuel E. West, so as to have enough for a small farm." The property, which cost $305, fronted on the Edgartown Road, a short distance east of the village of West Tisbury. Farthest inland of Vineyard villages, away from sight and sound of the sea, West Tisbury was favored by retired whaling captains and whalemen seeking to forget past voyages. It was also the agricultural center of the island.

Slocum's house, still standing, looks very much as it did when he left it. In 1965, the Dukes County Historical Society sponsored the placing of a bronze plaque in front of this, Slocum's only home on land—"His Last Years Were Lived in This House."

The Slocum house lay next door to the big house where Captain James Cleaveland, a Vineyard whaleman, lived. His granddaughter, Dionis Coffin Riggs, wrote me, "Capt. Slocum lived in . . . a very old, small Cape Cod house and added a section without regard to architectural unity, putting a curving Japanese-temple type of roof over the front and beside the door the usual shells and chunks of coral of the seafaring man.

"My grandfather used to entertain a great many interesting men in the kitchen. I remember his bringing Capt. Slocum into the front part of the house and my aunt greeting him and saying to me. . . . 'This is Capt. Slocum who sailed around the world in the sloop *Spray*.' As I remember, he was a small wiry man, bald, with a pointed beard and very bright, small, piercing dark eyes. . . .

"Mrs. Slocum used to stay with us occasionally. She was quite firm in her determination never to go to sea with her husband again. . . ."

Garfield wrote me his father bought the old house because he liked the large timbers, and the knees which looked like the hold of a ship. As far as the land was concerned, he planned to raise fruit trees. Though Slocum appeared to be quitting the sea, he did not give up the sloop in which he had sailed around the world. So while he farmed in the town of West Tisbury, the *Spray* waited in Menemsha harbor in the adjoining town of Chilmark.

Slocum had barely finished his first spring planting when he received a letter from Clifton Johnson (1865–1940) of Hadley, Massachusetts, an illustrator, photographer, and writer. Johnson wanted to visit Slocum, take pictures, and write about him. "Shall be very glad to welcome you to the island," Slocum replied from Vineyard Haven, 29 July 1902. "The *Spray* will be at one of the many near by ports say, Vinyard Haven Woods Holl, Manimsha, or New Bedford according as the wind blows; Let me welcome you onboard at one of these places some day this week—I will keep you posted on her whereabouts, by wire, from each place when I arrive   Then you have heard of the old *Spray* and Sailing

Alone   She is a knowing old boat and it's great fun sailing her Would you like to take a spin in her? . . . Come and we'll have a treat together out of the sea"

Johnson's article, "Captain Joshua Slocum—The Man Who Sailed Alone Around the World in a Thirty-Seven-Foot-Boat," illustrated with four of his photographs of Slocum, appeared in *Outing* magazine, October 1902. For biographical data he had to depend on the captain, and so got scant pickings—no dates, few names or places, not a word of Virginia, dead eighteen years.

"The *Spray*, as I first saw her," Johnson wrote, "lay gently rocking in a little cove on the Massachusetts coast near Woods Hole. . . . There were other vessels about. . . . The *Spray* could not compete with them in grace and style, yet she had an attractive air of domesticity and was evidently built for a sea home suited to all seasons and all waters and not simply adapted to fair summer weather along shore. It was a pleasure to set foot on her and note her snug appointments. It was a pleasure to eat with Captain Slocum a rough and ready lunch that he deftly prepared in the little galley, and it was a pleasure when night came to bunk under a deck awning and sleep on board. But, best of all, was a sail the next morning in 'the old *Spray*,' as her owner affectionately calls her, from the mainland across to Martha's Vineyard. . . .

"His house is one of the most ancient on the island—an oak-ribbed ark of a dwelling with warped floors and tiny window panes and open fireplaces. Its aspect is at present rather forlorn and naked, but the captain knows how to wield the hammer and the saw, and will soon make it snug. In a single season he has become an enthusiastic agriculturist, is proud of his flourishing garden and would like to own and make fruitful all the land round about. . . . Martha's Vineyard looks to him like Eden, and it is likely the sea will know him no more. . . ."

As for the man, in unpublished notes made in August 1902, Clifton Johnson described Slocum as "lithe, nervous, energetic" and a man who "says he is going to be 'light on his feet as long as he can get around at all.'" Jotting down his impressions, Johnson wrote that Slocum "has a temper and explodes like a firecracker when he is affronted. . . . Likes to relate his experiences and observations. Wags his head and gestures and sometimes acts out bits. In company may give you a knowing wink if on familiar terms. Hair and beard tinged with gray, head bald, but he looks 10 yrs younger than he really is. Keen gray eyes under bushy brows. Never loses his head in an emergency." *

Johnson saw Slocum in the first fine flush of farming. Garfield wrote that though he himself spent three years on the island, he did not help his father, and that all he recalled of the captain's agricultural efforts was the setting out of fruit trees.

Slocum's brother Ornan, who kept a shoe shop in Vineyard Haven, went to West Tisbury to help his brother, a relative wrote me. Apparently Slocum had little patience with Ornan. Despite constant bickering they worked together till the day when Ornan, while cultivating, ran (or let the horse run) against the trees. This barked them up and enraged the captain. He swore that Ornan was trying to wreck his beautiful young trees out of sheer cussedness. Ornan left, and he and the captain did not see each other again for some time. Then, one day, they met on a narrow path. They were ready to pass, eyes straight ahead, when Ornan thought what a couple of fools they had been, so he gave his brother the shoulder, and spinning him half way around, shouted with a grin, "Good morning, Captain!" So the incident ended happily enough but, Ornan did no more farming with his brother.

Clifton Johnson wanted to make another trip to West Tisbury to get material for another article. Slocum wrote him on 21 September from Rudder Ranch, West Tisbury.

My dear Mr Johnson
    I was delighted to hear from you again. . . .
    We will be able to put you up at our old ranch and be glad of the opportunity to do so, if you will take pot luck with us.
    My son Victor—just home from a whaling voyage—is helping me repair the shack. He is quite a sailor. Altogether we may fit the Spray on a voyage when you come. Please keep the lecture enterprise in view. . . .

Slocum must have been in a buoyant or playful mood when he headed his letter Rudder Ranch. Hettie told me he called the West Tisbury place Fag End; fag end, the untwisted end of a rope, a worn, useless ending.

* Clifton Johnson's manuscript notebook, "Captain Slocum," found among his papers in 1965, was loaned me by his son, Roger Johnson.

Johnson's second article on Slocum, "The Cook Who Sailed Alone," appeared in *Good Housekeeping*, February 1903. Slocum happened to be in New York on the eve of its publication. He sent Johnson a note about lecture business, 20 January 1903, and added a P. S. "I see 'Good Cooking by—' up in all the Elevated cars. I often wondered, when a boy, if I would become famous and see my name on soap advertisements. But this, the *real thing*, is better still. J.S."

Slocum gave a benefit lecture for the Congregational Church in his newly adopted town. On 20 November, the West Tisbury correspondent exhorted *Gazette* readers: "Do not forget the lecture at Agricultural Hall on Thursday evening by Capt. Slocum entitled 'A Tour Around the World.' A rare treat is in store for our people." Perhaps Slocum gave them, as he penned on one of his circulars, "100 slides of places visited and of peoples met with on the voyage, savage and otherwise." Paying lectures, however, were becoming scarce. Clifton Johnson got his brother Henry, proprietor of Johnson's Bookstore, Springfield, Massachusetts, to act as Slocum's agent. In December, Slocum gave his lecture in Springfield but his style of talk had about run its course.

"About the expenses of the last venture," Slocum wrote Clifton Johnson from West Tisbury, 17 April 1903, "please let me know if we are behind and I will stump up. I had several dates fired at me toward the close of the season—windfalls

"I think the titles of the talks shoud be especially for *Sunday* Sailing Alone; for other days: Reminscence of the Sea and Things I learned at Sea

"It should be easy enough to vary any of these subjects to suit time and place. Everything in connection with the sea should be eminantly respectable and be told in spirituality

"No man ever lived to see more of the solemnity of the depths than I have seen and I resent, quickly, a hint that a real sea story might be other than religeous

"I cannot down my sensativeness on this point."

For a short time earlier Slocum had been booked by the Lyceum Bureau of New York, and the leading impresario of the day, Major James B. Pond (1838–1903). For twenty-five years, Pond had handled such well-known names as Mark Twain, Cable,

Whitman, Stanley, Peary, Henry Ward Beecher, and William Dean Howells.

In his book, *Eccentricities of Genius,* the major explained that Slocum was born too late.

"Capt. Joshua Slocum, who conceived the idea that he could sail alone around the world, is about the newest and most remarkable of the small list of hazardous adventurers who have *done something that no other man has succeeded in accomplishing,* and thereby acquired world-wide fame. . . .

"What is most remarkable of all is that Captain Slocum is able to write and describe the incidents of the entire voyage and his wonderful experiences in a manner so graphic and simple that it absolutely charms and fascinates his hearers as few ever did or ever could do. . . .

"It is wonderful to listen to the descriptions of some of his hairbreadth escapes and to hear him answer, as quick as a flash, questions of every conceivable sort put to him by expert seafaring auditors. I have listened for hours to these seeming tournaments in navigators' skill, and never yet did the captain hesitate for an instant for a reply that went straight to the mark like a bullet. . . .

"Had all this occurred twenty years ago, it would have meant a fortune for Captain Slocum. . . ."

26

dangers there are, to be sure . . .
but the intelligence and skill
God gives to a man
reduce these to a minimum

Ten years with the *Spray* had worked Slocum out of debt and into a house and farm of his own, but he still seemed unable to settle down. During the winter of 1902–03, the West Tisbury correspondent of the *Vineyard Gazette* reported Slocum visiting Boston, New York, Washington, D.C., and North Carolina. There were even rumors the *Spray* might be shown at the St. Louis Fair, and that Slocum would return to Australia, but they had no discernible foundation.

Slocum wandered in and out of friends' and neighbors' lives. Each saw him in his own way, and remembered him as he saw him.

A relative in Boston recalled that one day the captain popped in unannounced, "by way of the kitchen," she wrote me, "with an enormous cod tucked under his wing with just a paper around its middle but the tail sticking out, and part of the other end where the head was happily off." Slocum had been up and down the waterfront, seeking out old acquaintances, and one of the fishermen had given him the specimen of his favorite food.

He told Clifton Johnson that when visiting friends, he was often asked to make a chowder; "and when I do get up one of my proper old-fashioned codfish chowders it brings them right to their feet," he said. "Why they were invalids before!" He said his method was so simple, and gave such appetizing results.

"Put some pork and a sliced onion in the pot and let that cook awhile," he explained. "Then put in a layer of potatoes and next a layer of fish, and so on up to the top with a seasoning of salt and pepper. Then add enough water to barely cover it and cook for twenty minutes. When it is about done put in milk and bits of crackers or bread and let it simmer a while. Your codfish must be cut in chunks and you must have the skin on it and the bones in it."

In the spring of 1903, the *Vineyard Gazette* reported that Slocum, in addition to his homestead, had purchased "a large wood lot and about 160 acres of cleared ground." He wrote Clifton Johnson, "My wife and I will be very glad of a visit from you at any time the sooner the better. I have about 160 acres of beautiful land. On some of the acres are stumps which I shall endeavor to hoist out putting in a hill of potatoes in its stead."

As is often the way with an enterprising but untried farmer, Slocum tried growing something new—in this case, hops. Flavel Gifford, who lived next door, remembered picking hops for Slocum at ten cents a pound, and how long it took to earn a dime, hops being light. Mrs. Donald Campbell of West Tisbury also picked hops for Slocum when she was a girl, but only once, for he did not repeat the experiment. He was, she said, "tall, spare, courteous, and reserved."

In his second summer on the farm, instead of making hay, Slocum went sailing on Buzzards Bay, and Vineyard and Nantucket Sounds. Edwin Robinson of Wentworth, New Hampshire, wrote me he saw the *Spray* hauled out at Onset, Massachusetts, in the summer of 1903; that he saw her again that summer at Cottage City, and rowed over to her. "Capt. Slocum was giving a young man a lecture on the proper way to come alongside an anchored boat without smashing up things. The captain said business of selling shells was slow but that he was going to stay around for a few days longer anyhow."

Dr. Charlotte Richmond of Amherst, Massachusetts, saw Slocum in the summer of 1903. "Capt. Slocum spent many weeks at Marion and my mother used to send me out in the rowboat with food supplies for him. In time I grew to regard him almost as a good uncle, a teller of wonderful tales, and a giver of many interesting small gifts," she wrote me.

When harvest time came, Slocum, instead of drying beans at home was hooking a shark at the Sippican Casino at Marion, "greatly to the relief of the bathers," the *Vineyard Gazette* reported.

As for Martha's Vineyard winters, Slocum did not like them. "I hope you will pardon my seeming neglect: I became so interested in trying to keep warm these winter days that I forgot all, except the wood-pile I have an oak grove, fortunately, near my house . . . ," he wrote to a friend, William H. Tripp, who had ordered a copy of *Sailing Alone*.

Many neighbors remembered Slocum. George G. Gifford, storekeeper and town clerk of West Tisbury for many years, recalled him as "not extremely tall nor extremely short, but a quite pleasant chap who talked with everybody. It was the general opinion," the storekeeper said, "that Slocum and his wife had separated—nothing legal—but just that he went his way and she went hers."

Another neighbor, Horace Athearn, called Slocum well-spoken and courteous. He described him as "a broad but lean and high-shouldered man who wore a close-cropped beard and was a great walker." According to Athearn, the peripatetic captain explored the whole island.

Still another Vineyarder, S. C. Luce, Jr., recalled the captain as slow moving and slow talking, "but," he said, "Slocum's head worked all right." Donald Campbell had a contrary impression. He thought Slocum's mind had been affected by the loss of the *Aquidneck*. Another resident of the village recalled the captain as "eccentric."

Joseph Chase Allen said that he knew Slocum the way a boy knows a man; that during the years Slocum was at the Vineyard, he (Allen) lived in Chilmark with his uncle, Fred Mayhew, who drove the stage coach. "I remember driving down with him one evening to meet the boat," Allen said. "The stage was just like a box and not too well made—all windows and doors. For the return trip, a rather well dressed woman took the middle seat and then a man got aboard and took the seat clear aft in the doggone box. I was up on the front seat with my uncle—we were headed up-island in the usual way—when all of a sudden I heard a hell of a rustle of paper. The man leans forward and says to the woman, 'I hope you don't object to the smell of salt codfish.' I looked around and he had the biggest jackknife I ever saw in my life, and he was hewing chunks off the fish, and eating, and he ate a good deal of the way to West Tisbury. That was Slocum in 1904.

"He looked a lot like other men of his generation who had been to sea—whiskery, very quick in his movements, and inclined to be snappy in his speech as men will be who are accustomed to give orders. He was not the kind of man one would be tempted to take liberties with. Only the women didn't think too highly of a man who stayed away from home so much without any particular objective."

Allen recalled the *Spray* tied up at Menemsha Creek, seven miles up-island from West Tisbury. He said Slocum carried on deck a small round bottom boat "chock full of all kinds of junk," and alongside the companionway, a Chinese gong and beside it, a wood hammer hanging from a silk rope. Allen said the captain's topping lift * was a very white native grass rope, and that a coil of the same kind of rope lay on one of the houses.

Ornan Slocum, who lived to a very old age, liked to tell about his brother. One day, so the story goes, he and Slocum went sailing in the *Spray* out of Vineyard Haven. The captain set the course too close to the rocks around West Chop. Ornan, who was at the wheel, warned that they were in danger, but his brother was calling the orders. When, finally, Slocum realized that he really was in too close, he shouted in a voice like the last trumpet, "Hard over!" Ornan responded with such sudden and vigorous action, that the captain fell full length on the deck, flat on his back. That was too much to take from Ornan. The captain sprang to his feet and made for him, but Ornan stood his ground. "Now wait, Josh, you gave the order and I obeyed," he said. Slocum admitted it. Then Ornan, pressing his luck, added, "Josh, I'm a happy man this day. All my life I've wanted to land you on your back and now, by gum, I've done it."

In his brief spell of farming, Slocum could not have made money; more likely he lost. Unsuited to the soil, he perhaps succeeded no better in this respect than his father. After 1904 he did little or no farming.

By the summer of 1905, Hettie began to take paying guests

* A rope and block by which the outer end of a boom is hoisted or supported.

while the captain lived a more private life in the sloop off the coast of Maine.

At the end of August 1905, Slocum was reported back home after a six months' leave. On 21 September the *Vineyard Gazette* said, "Capt. Joshua Slocum, accompanied by Mrs. Slocum, has been out on a fishing expedition in the sloop *Spray*." Apparently, Hettie was trying once more to become a seagoing wife; the captain, to become a fisherman. But the life was wrong for Hettie, and Slocum was wrong for fishing. A week later, when he turned up in Newport, Hettie had been replaced by a cat.

"There is nothing fancy about this animal," a newsman reported, "no pedigreed feline, just plain cat, but it makes a good companion. . . . His (Slocum's) boat is his house, and he spends most of his time in her. . . ." After renewing his license as a master mariner, the captain told the inquiring reporter that he was bound west to pick up his wife for a winter in southern waters.

So far as Hettie was concerned, however, the plan to go south in the *Spray* fell through. In October, she and Slocum made separate trips to Boston which resulted in their making separate arrangements. The captain went to live on the *Spray* while the *Vineyard Gazette* announced, "Mrs. Joshua Slocum has gone to Boston and expects to remain there most of the winter."

For some years the Smithsonian had been after Slocum to relieve them of the *Liberdade* for the Institution no longer had room for it. Slocum had tried several times to come to grips with the problem. In June 1905 he had written again to Otis Tufton Mason.

The *Liberdade*, as a boat, has gone—Her planks however and her ribs would be worth saving. Her sides are cedar—long lengths—I intended to have been in Washington long before this with a hacksaw and cut all the nails and bundle the old boat up for some reconstruction. . . .

If the old thing might be all sawd apart and bundled in some corner I would gladly send the amount of the cost and as soon as possible get the bundles away If not, let the executioner do his work I think you have been exceedingly patient and a friend. . . .

Now in the fall of 1905, before sailing south on the *Spray*, Slocum came up with another scheme. Instead of taking the *Liberdade* apart, he arranged to trade her off to Henry B. Davis, the last inhabitant of Noman's Land, a small island southwest of Martha's Vineyard. In exchange, Slocum was to get a share in a harbor Davis intended to open on Noman's.

From Menemsha, Martha's Vineyard, 7 November, Slocum wrote the Smithsonian, "The plan is to put power in the old Brazil boat and run her as a packet between Nomans and New Bedford —She will want some repairs I know, but one week on her will make things look different. . . ." The plan never went through. The harbor Davis projected did not get dredged, nor the *Liber-dade* delivered.

One of Slocum's friends at Menemsha was a man named Ernest J. Dean. Dean was a young trap fisherman, and having a boat with power, he also boated fish to New Bedford. He said that Slocum depended on him to tow the *Spray* in and out of Menemsha Creek, a worse tide hole then than now. He said that he and the aging captain, whom he greatly admired, spent hours together on the *Spray*, or on Dean's boat, or in Dean's boat-house.

The merchant captain who had sailed all seas discussed with his insular friend the forthcoming voyage. "It was most interesting and educational," Dean wrote me, "to lay out the proposed courses with him, and also amusing to see him run his index finger (I think every finger and thumb on both hands was knuckle busted, set back or crooked—they looked worse than the fingers of an old time ball player) over miles and miles of ocean chart, and listen to his running chatter of his experiences in different parts shown on the chart. . . ."

Some time in November 1905, Slocum, now past 60 and still sailing alone, left Menemsha, bound for the West Indies. Dean said the captain started in a hard norther so as to get out into the Atlantic trade winds as soon as possible. Slocum sailed south by easy stages, and called at Cuban and Jamaican ports. In Kingston, he was entertained by the colonel of the Royal Artillery in the style he had been accustomed to when going around the world. From there he sailed to Cayman Brac, then to Grand Cayman where he stayed two months. He called the country "delightful," and winter there, "very pleasant."

The sloop lay behind the reefs where Slocum spent his time in fishing up conch shells. The natives dived for them in two fathoms of water bringing up one at a time. Slocum, remembering the Vineyard quahog rake, rigged up a similar contraption and with it scooped up a dozen at once.

By the time he was ready to return to Massachusetts, Slocum had shipped about a thousand shells, together with such curiosities as specimens of the lace tree. Then just before he sailed, in early spring, several local admirers of Theodore Roosevelt asked him to deliver a half dozen rare orchid plants to the president. Slocum agreed to do so.

27

I was destined to sail
once more into the depths
of solitude ... a spirit
of charity and even benevolence
grew stronger in my nature

Slocum left Grand Cayman about 1 April. Bound for home, he detoured up the Delaware River and tied up opposite northeast Philadelphia, at the Riverton, New Jersey, Yacht Club where he had been invited to lecture. He also intended to visit Leslie W. Miller and his son, Percy Chase Miller, who summered at Martha's Vineyard but lived in Philadelphia.

Percy Chase Miller told me that he and his father regarded Slocum as an upstanding, rather strong character wearing what seemed, even then, old-fashioned chin whiskers. "Anyone brought into contact with the old man would have been interested in his general nautical appearance and atmosphere. There was no mistaking he was an old sea dog.

"He spent a night with us. He arrived respectably, and even nattily arrayed. I remember him saying he'd like me to play the piano for him, and I did—for an hour or more. He seemed to enjoy it; said the sounds were not unpleasing.

"Slocum was lean and hungry looking and gaunt. But he looked as though he could take care of himself. I never was disappointed in his appearance or behavior though I am quite sure he was a little cracked.

"I also saw him near Camden sometime in 1906. After he got

into trouble there, I felt he was a little dippy. He was put in jail and my father went to try and help him."

The trouble Miller referred to was published in a number of papers including the *Boston Herald* but not, apparently, in the *Vineyard Gazette*. At Riverton, a twelve-year-old girl went aboard the sloop. A few hours later, the girl's father claimed she had been attacked. The authorities charged Slocum with rape.

The weekly *New Era of Riverton and Palmyra, New Jersey*, 1 June 1906, page 2, published, "Held on Serious Charge." Naming the daughter of local residents, the paper said she "had suffered indignities at the hands of Capt. Slocum aboard his yacht *Spray*" on the previous Friday. "From the story of the child and an investigation by Dr. Mills, it became evident that the worst fears of the parents were not realized, the child not being injured, though she suffered considerably from nervousness." The incident is said to have occurred about three in the afternoon, while at five, the paper reported, Slocum went off to Philadelphia, doubtless to see the Millers.

"The Captain returned about nine o'clock in the evening," the paper continued, "and was arrested by Marshal Quigley. He was given a hearing before Recorder Coddington Saturday morning and committed to the county jail without bail. At the hearing Capt. Slocum said he had no recollection of the misdemeanor with which he is charged, and if it occurred it must have been during one of the mental lapses to which he was subject.

"The sloop *Spray* was placed in charge of Michael Faunce pending other arrangements. . . .

"Yesterday Judge Gaskill set Capt. Slocum's bail at $1,000." That is, bail was set six days after the captain's arrest.

The paper also published a letter written by the father of the girl wherein he said that an article entitled "An assault on a little girl in Riverton, N.J." appeared to misstate the facts, and that he and his wife "are greatly relieved to learn by questioning the child, also by Dr. C. S. Mills' examination, that there was no attempt at rape for the child is not physically injured although greatly agitated by the indecent action and exposure of the person on the part of this creature now posing in the limelight of cheap notoriety.

"We regret exceedingly the necessity of publicity for the child's sake but feel assured that the exposure of such a fiend will be regarded as a service rendered the public.

"We respectfully request you to publish this in a prominent place in your paper, for the interest of my child and family demand it."

The girl's father's letter did not save Slocum from being locked up on a charge of rape in the jail at Mt. Holly. He did not have a thousand dollars for bail. My search of the County Clerk's Office of Burlington County disclosed neither receipt for bail nor record of an indictment. Indeed, being all alone, the aging traveler would seem to have been at a disadvantage in obtaining full consideration of the law.

Held in an ancient stone jail, Slocum waited day after day for grand jury action which never came. Instead, his case was heard by a judge without jury—but not right away. The authorities seemed not to know what to do about their distinguished but somewhat unraveled caller.

Slocum was penned up 42 days. Jail was not like a boat but there were two things about it that he had long been used to—confinement and discomfort. As for patience, which he called the greatest of virtues, he had learned it from sailing.

The end of the unscheduled stopover in Slocum's long voyage home came on Friday afternoon, 6 July, when Judge Joseph H. Gaskill held another session of court. The charge had by now been changed to committing an indecent assault. Slocum's counsel entered a plea of *non vult contendere* (literally, he will not contest it) for his client, and said there was no intention to do the child bodily harm.

By this method, Judge Gaskill quietly put the case to rest. In winding up, he was reported as saying: "I am very sorry to be obliged to administer reproof to a man of your experience and years, and I am glad, and no doubt you are, too, that in this case there was no attempt made to injure the person of the girl. Upon request of the family I can deal leniently with you. You must never return to Riverton either by rail or water. By payment of all costs you are discharged."

Slocum got under way the next morning. Early in August he

put into Oyster Bay Harbor to deliver the sole surviving orchid to President Theodore Roosevelt. Archibald Roosevelt, one of the president's sons, sailing in the Harbor, came alongside.

"I was sailing around with a sailor from the president's yacht, the *Sylph*, who was named Obie," Archibald Roosevelt wrote me years later, "when we saw a decrepit looking old sloop, with the name *Spray* painted on it. On boarding her, Captain Slocum greeted us. He was a slim, medium-sized man, dressed in black trousers and a white shirt, and he took us around the boat, and told us yarns about his trip.

"When I went home that evening, I told my father of my visit, and he, since he had heard of the voyage, was very much interested, and asked me to go out the next day and extend an invitation to the captain to visit Sagamore Hill. This I did, and in due course the captain arrived, where he proceeded to make friends of all of us, particularly my brother Kermit, and me. He was fond of Kermit because he and Kermit were great admirers of the poems of Rudyard Kipling. The captain could repeat much of Kipling. I remember that he liked 'The Rhyme of the Three Sealers,' 'The Bell Buoy,' 'The Long Trail,' and 'The Virginity.'"

Slocum had navigated in a matter of days from a cell in a Jersey jail to a place as guest of the president. Archibald and Obie sailed with him to Newport, on board the *Spray*, while President Roosevelt wrote Henry Cabot Lodge, 6 August, ". . . Archie is off for a week's cruise with Captain Joshua Slocum—that man who takes his little boat, without any crew but himself, all around the world."

As for the week's cruise, Archibald Roosevelt wrote me, "The boat was the most incredibly dirty craft I have ever seen. You can imagine how it offended Obie, who had been trained in the U.S. Navy. When we stopped at New Haven, Obie went ashore, and returned with a kerosene stove, which he bought with his own money, and jettisoned the filthy old relic that had served the captain, I don't know how many years.

"In mild warm weather, the captain often cooked on deck, and he had a most ingenious contrivance. He had an old-fashioned laundry tub, in the bottom of which he coiled a piece of heavy anchor chain. On top of the chain he built a fire of drift-wood.

"As a diet, he was fond of salt fish and every so often he would make us enormous pancakes, 'as thick as your foot,' he would tell us.

"The sleeping quarters were in the after cabin, and Obie and I slept on the top of a wooden chest, and the captain had his bunk.

"In the hold, there was a quantity of miscellaneous equipment, and an enormous number of conch shells. Some of these had not been too carefully cleaned, and there was a fine ripe odor permeating the center part of the ship.

"While we were sailing, we would busy ourselves filing the points off the shells, and thereby making fog horns out of them. These, the captain would sell to visitors who came aboard when he was anchored in a port. He also sold his book, and charged, I believe, ten cents to every visitor. We learned, under his tutelage, to be pretty good salesmen of the shells and the book.

"Of course we saw the famous alarm clock, which had to be boiled before it would run. Beyond my comprehension were his sheets of calculations for the lunar observation he had made single-handedly—a feat, I believe which is supposed to require three people to work out.

"It is quite common for sail boats to sail on the wind with little or no attention paid to the helm, but the old *Spray* was, so far as my experience goes, unique in the fact that it would sail off the wind as well as on, without it being necessary to mind the helm after the course was set."

The meeting with the Roosevelt family, the first of several, ended in a most cheerful fashion. The captain received a complimentary letter:

My dear Captain Slocum:

I thank you for your interesting volume, which you know I prize.

By the way, I entirely sympathize with your feeling of delight in the sheer loneliness and vastness of the ocean. It was just my feeling in the wilderness of the west.

Sincerely yours,
Theodore Roosevelt

After seeing Archie and Obie home, Slocum went home himself—for the first time in nine months or so. But after less than a month on the farm, he went off to New Bedford. He told the *New Bedford Standard* he wanted to be the first through the Panama

Canal, then under construction, and after that, sail to China and Japan "to demonstrate that it is an easy trip." The Canal, however, did not open until 1915, six years after Slocum last was heard from.

Meanwhile, something had to be done about the *Liberdade*. The Slocum-Smithsonian correspondence had been dragging along seven years, and the boat was still in Washington, still in the way. Another letter went off, this time from Providence, R.I., 13 October 1906.

My dear Professor Mason:

If it is not asking too much I would like very much to have *Liberdade* hauled away to some lot or down to the Potomac if any of your people know a place for here there or most any where. I would chance her, turned bottom up, under a tree, or alongside of a stone wall or fence. . . .

I have written Archie Roosevelt about *Liberdade*. If Archie cares for her please deliver to him. Otherwise she might be hauled inland to some farm yard. I headed for Washington last spring but was blown off shore and couldn't fetch the capes of the Chessapeake. I am now on the eve, almost, of another trip to West Indies—It is glorious there in winter—and I will fetch the Potomac, in the Spring. . . .

Now the old craft at a farm house, if Archie dont want her, would be all right

I feel guilty for not having carted this boat away and after you have been so kind I have no right to ask it but if your people can lodge her somewhere for me till next Spring! Anyhow she must go from the present place.

Very Sincerely
Joshua Slocum

Later in the year Slocum arranged to have the *Liberdade* moved from the Smithsonian to a boat-yard on the Washington waterfront; but exactly where, or when, or what became of the *Liberdade,* no one knows.

28

you must then know the sea,
and know that you know it,
and not forget that it was made
to be sailed over

Slocum's literary career ended with publication of *Sailing Alone Around the World.* He wanted to write for the *Century* again but did not really have a subject. He thought of doing an article on a South Sea pirate, Bully Hayes, whom he knew of from merchant shipping days. He wrote Buel in February 1900, "Herewith is the best I can do for the moment. . . . I am expecting any day some data concerning him from Samoa, such as the schooner's name and the year he was murdered. . . . Will you pleas look Hayes over and send him a good wish. I have seen no one resemble him, in portrait, more than John Ruskin."

A month later Slocum wrote Buel again, "Of all the buccaneers and pirates of my acquaintance captain, pirate Hayes had the most winning ways—he was very taking   I may not do him justice but will send a sketch of him along tomorrow. . . ." If Slocum ever sent the sketch, Buel did not buy it.

Two years later, in April 1902, Slocum and Buel discussed the possibility of a new edition of *Voyage of the Liberdade* though the book did not suit Buel as it stood. Slocum mailed Buel the manuscript and wrote him, "I will strengthen human sympathy in it as I go along on the next trip through the MS—with a pilot onboard." But the Century Company did not reissue *Voyage of the Liberdade,* nor did any American book publisher until 1958 when Rutgers University Press included it in *The Voyages of*

Joshua Slocum.* After the Century Company rejected it, Slocum sold *Voyage of the Liberdade* to *Outing* magazine. *Outing* abridged it, gave it a new title—"The Voyage of the *Aquidneck* and Its Varied Adventures in South American Waters," and published it serially, November 1902 to April 1903.

All Slocum's best writing had been done in a ten-year period, 1889–1899, between the ages of 45 and 55. Probably in late 1905, or early 1906, he sold the last of his literary wares, the notes on Bully Hayes. In March 1906, *Outing* published "Bully Hayes, the Last Buccaneer. Written from Data Supplied by Captain Joshua Slocum." This was a ghostwritten piece indeed, and a strictly commercial transaction.

In autumn 1906, after putting in at New Bedford, Slocum cruised Buzzards Bay and Block Island Sound. The Slocum genealogist, Charles Elihu Slocum, M.D., looking for information, was having a hard time finding him. From Block Island, R.I., 15 November, Slocum replied briefly, "My mails have not reached me on time of late. . . . I regret that I have not been able to be, myself, a better subject among my kin—to have added an interesting line. . . ."

Slocum sailed south again, alone as usual, and spent a second winter in the Caribbean. Louise B. Ward, a Philadelphia newspaperwoman, saw him in Kingston, Jamaica, shortly after an earthquake on 14 January 1907 almost destroyed the city. "I went on the *Spray*," she wrote me in 1957, "and talked with him. He seemed well. I remember he said to me—'I can patch up the *Spray* but who will patch up Captain Slocum?' As I recall the boat it appeared fairly neat and clean though it did look old. Captain Slocum seemed like a quiet self-respecting New Englander with a normal voice and manner, though rather sad."

When spring came, Slocum spread his gray wings and headed north. From the banks of the Potomac, foot of Seventh Street, 26 May 1907, he wrote his second son, B. Aymar.

Dear Ben:

I was glad to get your letter. . . .

I am going ahead some again, with a vessel full of stuff worth something My books are selling rather better than at first

* *Voyage of the Liberdade* was published in 1948 in England by Rupert Hart-Davis.

I "lecture" Friday 31st at a fine hall here, and am promised a good house.

The president sent down for me yesterday to meet him in the Red Room, White House Archie came and brought me in their market wagon

Archie will join me again at Oyster Bay and come further east this summer, perhaps to Falmouth or Woods Hole. You must find time to meet us in Aug

Your father
Joshua Slocum

The old market wagon is reserved for best friends always.

The story is told that when Slocum and Roosevelt shook hands in the White House, the latter said, "Captain, our adventures have been a little different." To which Slocum replied, "That is true, Mr. President, but I see you got here first."

Archibald Roosevelt said his father took a great interest in Slocum as he did in all adventurous men, and entertained him at home rather than at the office. "I remember that my father rang for the butler," Archibald Roosevelt wrote me, "a wonderful old colored man named Duncan, and ordered a rum drink for the captain. When the captain protested, my father explained that as he was only a president, while the captain was a real captain, he (the captain) would have to drink for both of them. After the visit, I rode back to the Navy Yard with Slocum, and he said to me: 'My head is just humming from that drink!' It was only years later that I found that he was practically a teetotaler."

From Washington, Slocum sailed to Oyster Bay. When he arrived, in June, the presidential yacht was moored at the harbor entrance. Overlooking the harbor was Sagamore Hill, the summer White House. He anchored alongside a Sandy Hook pilot boat, owned by a young man, Stanley Putney Morris. Morris wrote me he helped tow the *Spray* into nearby harbors "where the captain gave talks to various groups and sold and autographed a lot of books. . . . He had a very nice Columbia phonograph . . . would play records and spin yarns."

Slocum waited around Oyster Bay for young Archibald. They were planning a second trip together. "Once a year sea-battered, kindly old Capt. Joshua Slocum puts in the harbor here with his weatherbeaten snub-nosed, tight little yawl, the *Spray*. . . . to see his chum, Archie Roosevelt. The two are fast friends and they are preparing to start Monday for a cruise along the New England coast. . . ." reported the *New York World,* 13 July. But the second trip never came off.

That fall, however, Slocum showed up at Groton, "on a Sunday to call on my brother, Kermit and me," Archibald Roosevelt wrote me. Groton was a strict Episcopalian school, and the captain, like the other guests, was expected to attend chapel, and afterwards to shake hands with the rector—which he did. The Roosevelt boy stood by his friend while the rector politely asked how the visitor enjoyed the service. "Well," replied the captain who had personal ideas on communion with his Maker, "there was too much popping up and setting down, and too much sassing back!"

Plans for sailing with Archibald having fallen through, Slocum returned to Martha's Vineyard alone. Arriving at Cottage City (Oak Bluffs) at the height of the summer season, he soon found a little crew eager to help him unload. One of the former hands said that she was a girl of twelve when she met Slocum in the summer of 1907.

"His boat was tied up at the wharf," Mrs. Carroll W. Saley wrote me, "and my girl chum and I were fascinated with the sponges, shells, and odd things he had for sale. He was friendly and told us all about them. . . . When he found that we were at the Frasier House, just over the rise, he asked us if we would like to sell his little souvenir books, shells, etc. . . . We were delighted. . . . We learned the stories and where the articles came from, and how to blow the shells for customers as the captain did when he needed a fog horn. He was much pleased with our work, and paid us well . . . and was kind to us always."

In an article, "Nova Scotia to Martha's Vineyard: Notes on Captain Joshua Slocum," published by Dukes County Historical Society, August 1969, David T. Hugo wrote, "There is no question that Joshua was a bit odd. Doris Marshall of Vineyard Haven tells of going to visit the *Spray* and her captain at Oak Bluffs. She and a girl friend had brought along a bunch of nasturtiums by way of introduction. After pleasantries, the Captain said that the nasturtiums 'would be his greens for the day.' Mrs. Marshall says he then proceeded to eat the bouquet." This may have seemed odd but nasturtium flowers are sometimes eaten in salads; the plant's other name is Indian cress. Evidently Slocum knew the arts of living off the land as well as the sea.

Continuing with these recollections, Hugo wrote that Slocum "read them something from a book in braille, saying he had taught himself so he could read when it was impossible to keep a candle going on the boat. If true this was quite a little extra for the Captain. The girls certainly were impressed."

Impressing young visitors by reading in braille was, I suspect, an example of Slocum's humor. Clifton Johnson's unpublished manuscript of August 1902 noted, "*Sailing Alone* in two great volumes raised printing for the blind."

Writing in the *Vineyard Gazette*, 24 June 1966, Phillips N. Case told of seeing Slocum at Cottage City harbor in the early 1900s. "The *Spray* was entirely too big and clumsy to sail out through the narrow channel between the jetties in anything but a fair wind," Mr. Case wrote, "but when it was very calm Captain Slocum had another expedient. For such conditions, not only at Cottage City but in close quarters anywhere in the world, the captain kept a long, slender pole lashed on deck. When the occasion arose, he would go forward to the bow and, planting one end of the pole in the bottom of the channel, grasp the other end, pushing on it as he walked to the stern, moving the boat ahead. Then he would repeat the operation as often as necessary until the boat was out of the harbor."

In the fall of 1907, Slocum made his third trip south alone. Vincent Gilpin (1875–1962), author and yachtsman, saw him in January 1908 in Miami, then a very small town. Gilpin bought a copy of *Sailing Alone* and went to hear Slocum lecture—so he wrote me almost 50 years later, and added these recollections of Slocum.

I rather think he lived on the *Spray*. . . . He was thrifty and usually hard up—which didn't bother him for his wants were few. *Spray* . . . was very simply fitted out, rather bare, and very damp from many soakings with salt water, and Slocum kept a little wood-stove going to help dry her out. I remember seeing him lunching one day on what looked like a half-baked potato from which he sliced pieces with his jack-knife. He was rather shabbily dressed in civilian clothes, with a ragged black felt hat. . . . On the whole, I felt him a good example of the old-line Yankee skipper, competent, self-reliant, not talkative, but perfectly friendly and ready to answer questions. He was obviously a first-class boat-handler—which is something quite different from being a ship-captain: apparently he was both, beside being a ship-wright. A very capable man; and a lonely, unhappy man.

Slocum knew his Vineyard friend, Ernest Dean, was working in the Bahamas as captain of a yacht. One day Slocum turned up in Nassau harbor. Dean saw him right away. In a letter to me years later, Dean said, "I had one of my sailors row me alongside, and when Slocum recognized me, he let out a loud, 'Come aboard!' grabbed me by the arms and fairly swung me on deck. I was amazed (and still am) at his strength. . . ."

In Nassau, Slocum made one of his last appearances on the plat-form. Dean recalled it as "a soup and fish" affair at the Colonial Hotel. The governor and his staff attended. After the talk, the captain was kept busy telling more yarns in the grille, where the men, according to Dean, became hilarious and liberal. The captain went away $460 to the good. A few nights later he gave his talk in a church for an admission fee and took in $42.

Dean recalled a further incident of the captain's visit. It showed how hypersensitive Slocum had become. Dean said he was walking on Bay Street when he saw the sloop lying alongside a sponge wharf, and four or five natives standing in a group, and Slocum standing between them and the edge of the wharf. One native was holding a cloth over his mouth which was bleeding. "Slocum," Dean wrote, "seemed all nerved up. I asked him what had hap-pened, and here is his reply:

" 'I was splicing some rigging on deck when they came along —ginned up some—and started talking about the *Spray* and its size and running it down in general. One of them said loud enough for anyone to hear, "Any mon that says he sailed around the world in that thing is a goddom liar." I looked up in time to see which one said it, made a pier head leap, and with a couple of side-winders, unshipped his jaw.' "

Late in the following spring, on 11 May 1908, Hettie wrote her husband's friend, Buel. She said she had read that the *Spray* had been lost. "Personally have not heard from Captain Slocum since Nov. 1st 1907. . . . Will you kindly yet me know if you have heard from him or of him of late. . . ." But Buel had had no word either.

On 2 June, Slocum sailed into New York harbor with a two-ton chunk of coral on board for the American Museum of Natural History. It had been found by scientists off Andros Island in the Bahamas, and they had engaged the ex-merchant captain to transport it to the United States. It was the tenth anniversary of the return of the *Spray*.

Though Slocum must have been pleased to be carrying cargo again, he had left the West Indies in a huff. He had heard remarks among the governor's staff which were, or he thought were, uncomplimentary to the *Spray* and himself. So when the governor asked to see the coral he was taking out of the country, Slocum did not comply. Instead, when ready to leave, he beat the *Spray* up to the channel entrance buoy directly below the hill on which the governor's residence stood. Then swinging the *Spray* off before the wind, he presented the governor with a fine view of her broad stern. In his heightened state of exasperation, he was making the nautical equivalent of a vulgar gesture.

The two-ton coral tree Slocum carried stands deep in the Museum's coral forest, a replica of a coral reef, in the Hall of Ocean Life. Along with the coral, Slocum presented the Museum with a gift from himself—a wooden shield from North Queensland, Australia. This too is in the Museum of Natural History's collection.

In a note thanking him for bringing the coral, the Director, Hermon Carey Bumpus, said he was sending Slocum a photograph of the south façade of the Museum. From Vineyard Haven, 23 July, Slocum replied, "I am more than pleased with the thought of having the picture in the Spray library, and it shall together with your letter, find a prominent place in this part of the Old sloop where treasures are to be found."

By the summer of 1908, Slocum, in his adopted town, was recognized as the transient he had become. On 30 July, the *Vineyard Gazette* said "Captain Joshua Slocum of the sloop *Spray* is on the Island and has been a recent guest of Mrs. Slocum at West Tisbury." The *Vineyard Gazette* mentioned Slocum only twice again in his lifetime. On both occasions it reported him on the move.

29

I was born in the breezes,
and I had studied the sea
as perhaps few men
have studied it,
neglecting all else

The last time Archibald Roosevelt saw Slocum was in Oyster Bay again, in cooler weather, probably late in 1908. "The *Sylph* was taking my father and the family to some function or other," he wrote me, "and had just weighed anchor and was rounding the Light House, when we saw the *Spray* beating into the harbor. Of course the men were all busy and failed for several minutes to see that the *Spray* had dipped her flag in salute to the president. When we returned, and called on the *Spray*, the captain of the *Sylph* apologized and gave as an excuse the explanation that they were so busy. Captain Slocum laughed: 'I held those halliards till I thought my hands would freeze. There were fifty men on the *Sylph* and one on the *Spray*, but evidently that one can get things done on time.'"

Around 1908, H. S. Smith, who had spotted the *Spray* on her way to Newport ten years earlier, paid the usual admission fee and went aboard the sloop in New Bedford. He explored her thoroughly. On going below, he found "many evidences of serious deterioration," he wrote me in March 1953.

Smith and his companions went for a sail with the captain. "We were all allowed a trick at the wheel," Smith said, "and I was amazed at the old tub's easy steering and her dryness. There was a strong southwesterly blowing which raised the usual Buzzards

Bay chop, but not a drop of water came aboard and she sailed at a
remarkably small angle of heel. Also, once sheets had been properly trimmed, she would steer herself for an indefinite time, to
such an extent that a trick at the wheel was rather monotonous
and somewhat unnecessary."

Smith described Slocum as wearing a battered felt hat, "originally black but bleached out irregularly," a collarless shirt, a vest,
unbuttoned trousers, and high lace-up shoes "badly in need of
polish." The captain volunteered little information but readily
answered questions. "His language was that of a cultured gentleman," Smith said; and he spoke rather vaguely of a possible voyage
down the east coast of South America.

But, Smith added, the *Spray* was dirty. "Not just a little dirty
but very, very dirty." He said that the captain was much run
down physically, "and perhaps mentally," and that he was exceedingly indifferent to his surroundings.

West Tisbury had lost its charms for Slocum. On 4 September
1909, he wrote Victor.

Your letter . . . received just as I was leaving W Tisbury
. . . We are pulling out of it for the winter at least and would sell
if a purchaser should turn up. . . .
I am on the *Spray* hustling for a dollar
Just where I will be next I don't know. . . .

Slocum was not exaggerating; he did not know where he might
be next. Sixty-five years old, he was dreaming up a tremendous
voyage. It was to turn out to be his last. His plan was to sail to
Venezuela, sail up the Orinoco River into the Rio Negro, thence
to the headwaters of the Amazon. He would then sail down the
greatest of rivers to the ocean, and so on home. He planned to go
alone as usual but this time equipped with a phonograph so that
if Indians mistook him for a god, he would not disappoint them.

In his book about his father, Victor Slocum wrote that Slocum
took the *Spray* to the Herreshoff Works at Bristol, Rhode Island,
for an overhaul and that when she left "she was well fitted and
provided for." Slocum himself, Victor wrote, "was in the best of
physical health."

L. Francis Herreshoff wrote me years later, "The *Spray* did not have any work done on her at the Herreshoff Company but simply lay at one of their wharves in what is called Walker's Cove. She may have been given some old ropes, but the captain did everything himself in the refit. In my opinion the *Spray* was a poor boat for single-handed cruising. . . . some of her gear was very light and weak. . . . I shouldn't be surprised if I were the last one to speak to the captain for I saw him off on the morning that he departed."

Herreshoff, however, seems not to have been the last. From Bristol, Slocum returned to Menemsha. Vineyarders watched him preparing to sail. Some said he would plant his bones in that boat.

Captain Ernest Mayhew of Menemsha told me he thought Slocum had been getting slack; that just before he sailed, the *Spray* had been moored by two stakes; that high tide had lifted her bowsprit onto one of the stakes, and that when the tide fell, the bowsprit was hung up on the stake and lifted several inches. Captain Mayhew said that to his astonishment all Slocum did was take an axe and drive the bowsprit back into place.

Ernest Dean of Chilmark thought that the *Spray* and Slocum had grown old together. He told me that when he first met Slocum and the *Spray,* "they both were neat, trim, and seaworthy, but as the years rolled along there were signs of wear and exposure." Captain Donald LeMar Poole, who went aboard the *Spray* when he was a boy, reminisced, "her rigging was slack and in need of tarring, and Irish pennants were much in evidence." Irish pennants are loose ends hanging from the sails or rigging.

From Menemsha, Slocum sailed to Vineyard Haven. After securing the *Spray* in the harbor, Slocum walked up to Main Street. At Bodfish and Call, the North End Grocery, he ordered four or five boxes filled with sea-going grub.

On 14 November 1909, Slocum set sail from Vineyard Haven in the Town of Tisbury, outward bound. Captain Levi Jackson of Edgartown told me he was coming in from codfishing off the Muskeget Channel shoals (between Martha's Vineyard and Nantucket) in his boat, the *Priscilla,* when he saw the *Spray,* bound out. At the time he remarked it looked bad for a boat without power to be heading southeast. The wind was coming from that direction and by evening it was blowing a gale. Captain Jackson said he had been glad to get home because during the night the gale hauled northwest making a heavy cross sea and whipping up great combers over the shoals.

Francis V. Mead of Boston wrote the *Vineyard Gazette* he believed he and Captain John Randolfe of Cottage City, fishing in Muskeget Channel, were the last to see Slocum.*

After leaving Vineyard Haven, Slocum seems not to have made his next port of call. He was not heard from again. No trace of the *Spray* was found.

Vincent Gilpin, the yachtsman who saw the *Spray* in Miami in 1908, pointed out that "her sails and rigging would have been renewed more than once, and would have always had weak spots. This alone . . . might have caused her loss. . . ."

H. S. Smith, who saw the *Spray* in the same year in Fairhaven, wrote that "*Spray's* planking was in poor shape. No two planks appeared to be of the same shape, size or thickness, or even of the same kind of wood." He described the *Spray* as a "slow, docile, seakindly craft that would take care of herself for days at a time, but the shape she was in would give the horrors to anyone who went to sea. It could be the captain took care of some of the neglect as soon as he quit the land, but there was nothing in the world he could have done for the way she had been roughly cobbled together in the first place." †

T. F. Day, editor of *Rudder* magazine, guessed the *Spray* threw off a plank. He wrote that the last time he saw her she was "considerably dozy." Victor Slocum believed that with her dim oil-burning running side-lights, the *Spray,* heading south, was cut down in the shipping lanes she would have to cross.

There were, and will be, theories as to what might have happened. There is always the possibility of the sailor falling, or being washed over the side. Since by his own account Slocum suffered occasional lapses of memory, he might have blacked out. Or a combination of causes, desires, and motives may have led to the end. Garfield told me his father said he hoped to be buried at sea. It is not unthinkable or even ironical that Slocum most likely

* B. H. Kidder of Oak Bluffs wrote the *Vineyard Gazette* that he saw Slocum later in Bridgeport, Connecticut, asked him where he was going, and that Slocum replied, "Some far away places." It does not seem likely, however, that the year was 1909.

† "Quite Another Matter" by H. S. Smith, *The Skipper,* March 1968.

was lost close to land. In *Sailing Alone Around the World* he wrote that the closest call in all the global voyage came on a trip across a lagoon in a squall. Whatever the surmise, the gale as Captain Levi Jackson recalled it should be taken into account, as should the dangerous shoals and currents between Martha's Vineyard and Nantucket. The condition of the *Spray* must be considered and, most of all, Slocum's state of being, physical and mental.

Hettie's petition to the Probate Court of Dukes County filed 22 April 1912 stated that Joshua Slocum "disappeared, absconded and absented himself on the 14th day of November A.D. 1909; . . . that the said absentee . . . a Master Mariner by occupation . . . disappeared on the date above-named under the following circumstances, to wit: He sailed from Tisbury Massachusetts in the Sloop 'Spray' of about nine tons burden only . . . encountered a very severe gale shortly afterwards and has never been heard from since. . . ."

The final voyage required years to reach a legal destination. On 15 January 1924, the court granted Hettie whatever her husband had left behind. Joshua Slocum was pronounced legally dead as of the date on which he last set sail.

30

"Remember, Lord,
my ship is small
and thy sea is so wide!"

Men still feel challenged to take small boats on voyages around the world. Many go single-handed; some write as well as sail. None, however, has made the voyage Slocum made. None has taken the extremely hazardous route through the Strait of Magellan and around the Cape of Good Hope. None has written a book like his which transcends the subject matter and has become a work of literature.

The story of Joshua Slocum is a story of faithfulness to calling. In the classical manner of venturers, he began life by leaving home early. He chose a lonely mode of existence, but the sea filled the hollow left by affection denied. For a few years he shared his life with the perfect companion. When she died, then he was left even more alone than before.

Slocum's passions were fierce. Though often outwardly serene, to the end of his life he was driven by human discontent and restlessness. A kind of prophet of the value of insecurity, he finally sailed away from a world in which he could find no place.

Men who follow the sea, particularly those who spend days, and months, and years at sea, without companionship, develop a philosophy not easily explained. Such a life suckles a type of man, ingrown, perhaps, but firm in his belief in himself and in God; supremely confident, but humble before the Lord on the great waters; purposeful and tenacious, and above all determined to go as his own beliefs lead him. A time may come to seek Joshua Slocum further, but for the present the search has ended.

Sources of Slocum Material

The chief sources of information on the life of Joshua Slocum are his books, his letters, contemporaneous newspaper and magazine accounts, and the recollections of those who knew him.

Books in Print, 1970, lists half a dozen editions of *Sailing Alone Around the World,* and two of *Voyage of the Liberdade. Voyage of the Destroyer* is available only in *The Voyages of Joshua Slocum,* Rutgers University Press, 1958, which includes Slocum's two other books as well. *The Voyages* presents all Slocum's letters in the Records of the Department of State (Record Group 59) in the National Archives, Washington, D.C.; also A Check List of Published Works of Joshua Slocum, A Note on Sources, and a Selected Bibliography.

Slocum's letters to Roberts Brothers are in the Library of the Peabody Museum, Salem, Massachusetts. His letters to Century Company editors are in the Century Collection, Manuscript Room, The New York Public Library. Those to persons at the Smithsonian Institution, Washington, D.C., are in the files of the Institution's Department of Engineering and Industries. All other letters and documents referred to are in my possession.

As for recollections of Joshua Slocum, they are getting harder to come by. Many of the persons I met or corresponded with who had known him, were old, and have died since. Slocum's second wife, Hettie, who I saw in West Tisbury, Massachusetts, in July 1952, died in October of the same year.

Victor, the oldest of Slocum's children, died in 1949. In September 1952, I began corresponding with B. Aymar Slocum; also with Jessie Slocum Joyce who signed her letters, "The

Captain's Daughter," and with J. Garfield Slocum. Garfield, who wrote me notes from his sickbed, died in January 1955. B. Aymar, whom I visited twice, died in April 1965. I lost track of Jessie.

My book, *The Search for Captain Slocum,* Charles Scribner's Sons, 1956, contained many notes indicating the sources for statements made. I saw no reason to repeat the notes here. Following the Scribner edition, it was published in England in 1959 by André Deutsch. Editions Chiron put out a French translation in Paris in 1964 under the title, *Slocum Homme de Mer.* An Italian language edition is forthcoming.

The photographs came from various persons. B. Aymar Slocum gave me a number of photographs and glass negatives of his father, three of his mother, and the photograph of Virginia's grave.

Clifton Johnson's photographs of Slocum were provided by his widow, Anna M. Johnson of South Hadley, Massachusetts, who died in 1954, and sons, Irving and Roger.

On 28 December 1952, *The New York Times Book Review* published my "Author's Query" saying that I was "studying Capt. Joshua Slocum . . . and would like to hear from those having pertinent letters, documents, recollections, etc." Winfield Scott Clime, a landscape artist living in Old Lyme, Connecticut, responded promptly. "When Captain Slocum was at one of the Washington, D.C. docks," Mr. Clime wrote me, "I saw him a number of times, and made some photographs of him . . . From 1904 to 1914 I was employed in the Illustration Section of the Bureau of Publications of the U.S. Department of Agriculture, and after 4:30 every afternoon I did much painting and sketching around the wharves, which at that time were picturesque. That is how I met Captain Slocum . . . I went down to see him often, and never met anyone else with him. It seemed to me he was always very sad . . . Below I saw a sextant, badly corroded. I asked him if it was a souvenir with a history, and he answered, with a smile, that it was the sextant he used on his trip . . . I am enclosing six photographs . . . which you may have copied and use as you wish. The negatives I cannot locate and these are the only prints I have."

Other pictures came as a result of two pieces I wrote about

Slocum; an article in the *Vineyard Gazette,* 19 June 1953, and an introduction to *Sailing Alone Around the World,* Sheridan House, New York, 1954. A photograph I liked very much was sent me in February 1955 by Charles L. Clapp, Quincy, Massachusetts. "I have one of the original edition of *Sailing Alone Around the World* which I bought some years ago in a second hand bookstore," he wrote. "The flyleaf is inscribed, 'Sailed Alone With God. I am with great respect, Joshua Slocum. Onboard the "Spray," Marion, August 15, 1903.' There is a photograph of Capt. Slocum pasted in the front showing him sitting on a bench under the boom of the sail, and inscribed, 'Captain Slocum on the Spray, Marion, Mass., August 16, 1903.' " This is the photograph I referred to in the Preface to the First Edition.

In 1961, I gave some Slocum photographs to the Peabody Museum, Salem, Massachusetts. Copies are available from the Museum on request.

I am indebted to all who helped. Some are named in the text; I wish I could have cited everyone. I am especially grateful to William Sloane, Director of Rutgers University Press.

Index

ABOUT THE AUTHOR

Walter Teller was born in New Orleans in 1910. He received his Ph.D. from Columbia University. Earlier he studied at Haverford College and Harvard University. He is a fellow of the John Simon Guggenheim Memorial Foundation and is the author of *Cape Cod and the Offshore Islands, Area Code 215: A Private Line in Bucks County, Five Sea Captains, The Voyages of Joshua Slocum, The Search for Captain Slocum: A Biography, An Island Summer, Roots in the Earth* (with P. Alston Waring), *The Farm Primer*. His essays have appeared in *The New York Times Book Review, The American Scholar,* and other publications.